THE LOOK OF SUCCESS

How to Make a First Impression That Counts!

James O. Stallings, M.D.
with Marcia Powell

Frederick Fell Publishers, Inc.
New York, New York

DEDICATION

To Rick Rayle, my best friend, staunch supporter, and most trusted advisor, without whom none of my literary efforts would have been accomplished.

Gracious acknowledgement is given for permission to reprint the following: The dental photographs on pages 180–183, and 187 copyright by the American Dental Association. Reprinted by permission. Drawings on pages 75 and 189 from A NEW YOU—*How Plastic Surgery Can Change Your Life* by Dr. James O. Stallings. Copyright © 1977 by JOS Enterprises Ltd. Reprinted by permission of Van Nostrand Reinhold Company. Photographs on pages 50, 51, and 113 courtesy of "Men's Hairstylist & Barber's Journal" copyright November 1981. Photographs pages 4–6, 10–12: Wide World Photos, Inc.; drawing page 33: *Modern Salon* magazine; drawings pages 35, 38, 39, 52 and 53 (top of each page), and 83: Sunkist; photographs pages 41 and 57; Jamaica Tourist Board; photographs pages 59, 60, 112, 114–118, 120, 128, 129, 148, 159, 169, and 170: Maybelline; photographs pages 68 and 69: Covermark; drawings and charts pages 78, 80, 81, 84, 99, and 100: Clairol; drawing page 86 and photograph page 95: Peter Hantz Company; photographs page 87: International Guild of Professional Electrologists Inc.; photographs pages 88, 90, and 91: National Hairdressers and Cosmetologists Association; photographs pages 99 and 101: Eva Gabor International; photograph page 109: Elfin Cosmetics, Inc., drawings pages 121–126: Max Factor; photographs pages 135–137: Optical Manufacturers Association; drawings pages 138 and 139: the American Optometric Association; photograph page 163: *Hearing Instruments* magazine; photograph page 184: Cherilyn G. Sheets, DDS.

International Standard Book Number: 0-8119-0456-3
Library of Congress Catalog Card Number: 82-71744

Copyright © 1982 by J.O.S. Enterprises Ltd.

For information address:
Frederick Fell Publishers, Inc.
386 Park Avenue South
New York, New York 10016

Published simultaneously in Canada by Fitzhenry & Whiteside, Limited, Toronto

Manufactured in the United States of America
1 2 3 4 5 6 7 8 9 0

Contents

Acknowledgments

Any book that covers such a broad range of information and specialties is made possible only through the efforts of many people. That is certainly true of *The Look of Success.*

Foremost in this effort were Marcia Powell and Merrick Scott Rayle. Marcia's creative, conceptual, interviewing, and writing expertise, combined with the knowledge gained through almost twenty years of experience as a journalist, spokesperson, author, and public relations executive enabled her to transform a preliminary idea into a polished presentation.

The other major role in the compilation of this book was that of my friend and attorney, Rick Rayle, whose advice, guidance, support, and coordination of this project were as essential as the skills of a director are to a successful play or film.

I also am most appreciative to Suzanne M. Henry for her research and editorial contributions, and to Betsy Meltzer for her assistance with our research. Thanks also are due to Cheri Pupp, who provided ideas as well as her expert typing skills, and to Diane Angerame, the talented artist who drew most of the illustrations.

Jean Adams of *Redbook* was a source of encouragement, ideas, and resources which were invaluable, and Vivian Manuel also contributed excellent ideas and much-appreciated support. My dedicated and hard-working office and hospital staff also deserve thanks.

To Wayne Smith, whose expertise in literary promotion I highly regard, I extend special appreciation for his efforts on my behalf. I also want to recognize the services of my accountant, Donald Briggs, and another legal advisor, Mary Ruth Ottoson.

For their cooperation in the use of their photographs, I thank Jo Anne Clark, Bill McHugh, Roger Fisher, and Doug Zane, and photographers Konstantin Pio-Ulsky, James T. Kascoutas, and Harold Nadeau.

I extend special thanks to the following professionals who so graciously consented to be interviewed for this book and to review portions related to their areas of expertise: Kay Acuazzo, President, Skin Care Association of America; Doctor Marlene A. Bevan, President, Academy of Dispensing Otologists; Anna Crispen, skin care specialist; Doctor Daniel M. Eichenbaum, Department of

Ophthalmology, Westchester County Medical Center; Karen Feld, freelance writer; Doctor Lee Graber, Associate Professor of Dentistry, Loyola University, and research scientist, American Dental Association Health Foundation; Peter Hantz, President, Peter Hantz Company; Doctor Ann C. Hill, Assistant Clinical Professor of Dermatology/Medicine, Cornell University Medical College; Fino Gior, President, International Guild of Professional Electrologists Inc.; Carole Jackson, author, *Color Me Beautiful*; Ann Keane, past President, Skin Care Association of America; Doctor Albert M. Kligman, Professor of Dermatology, University of Pennsylvania School of Medicine; Judith B. Kuriansky, Ph.D., Clinical Psychologist; Doctor Paul Lazar, Professor of Clinical Dermatology, Northwestern University Medical School, and President, Dermatology Foundation; Josef Scigliano (Mr. Josef), Vice-President, Eva Gabor International; Doctor Alan R. Shalita, Chairman, Department of Dermatology, State University of New York, Downstate Medical Center; Doctor Cherilyn G. Sheets, Fellow, Academy of General Dentistry; Doctor John R. Thompson, former Professor of Orthodontics, Northwestern University Medical School.

In addition, I wish to recognize the contributions of the following organizations and individuals: Academy of General Dentistry; Professor Gerald R. Adams, Ph.D., Department of Family and Human Development, Utah State University; American Academy of Dermatology; American Academy of Facial Plastic and Reconstructive Surgery; American Academy of Otolaryngology; American Association of Orthodontists; American Board of Plastic Surgeons; American Dental Association; American Egg Board; American Optometric Association; American Society of Plastic and Reconstructive Surgeons; Professor Ellen Berscheid, Ph.D., Department of Psychology, University of Minnesota; Clairol; Cosmetic, Toiletry and Fragrance Association; Helene Curtis Professional Division; Elfin Cosmetics Inc.; Max Factor and Company; United States Food and Drug Administration; *Glamour; The Hairstylist;* Robert Half International Inc.; *Hearing Instruments*; Jamaica Tourist Board; Professor Richard M. Kurtz, Ph.D., Department of Psychology, Washington University; Maryland Commission of Human Rights; Maybelline; *Modern Salon;* National Association to Aid Fat Americans, Inc.; National Commission on Working Women; National Hairdressers and Cosmetologists Association Inc.; National Hearing Aid Society; National Society to Prevent Blindness; Lydia O'Leary; Optical Manufacturers Association; *Playboy; Savvy;* Sunkist Growers Inc.; and *Working Woman.*

1
LET'S FACE IT

"Our own beauty or ugliness will not only figure in the image we get about ourselves, but will also figure in the image others build up about us and which will be taken back into ourselves."[1]

These observations by psychologist Paul Schilder are as apt today as when he first expressed them almost half a century ago. Although many of us don't like to admit it, we do judge—and are also judged—on the basis of appearance.

As we will see from the range of contemporary research presented later in this chapter, first impressions tend to be based on various preconceived ideas (primarily stored away in our subconscious) about certain relationships between appearance and qualities of character, intelligence, ability, and personality. Because it is our most visible asset, we focus on the face and instinctively make our initial deductions about those whom we are meeting based on what we see in their faces.

If we become better acquainted with an individual, we may learn that our first impression was incorrect. However, all of us are confronted to varying degrees with situations where, if the first impression isn't satisfactory, there will be no opportunity for a follow-up assessment. This is especially true in our business lives. In these situations, particularly, each of us wants to do whatever we can to ensure a response that will be to our benefit.

Few human beings are classically beautiful or handsome; however, we all have the potential to appear more attractive by making the best use of our physical assets and eliminating (or at least minimizing) our deficits. We can learn how to create a facial appearance that is consistent with the image we want to project to others. Sometimes achieving that image is as simple as more skillful application of makeup, a change of hairstyle or color, switching from eyeglasses to contact lenses (or vice versa), or more careful selection of clothing styles and colors.

In other cases, more serious changes may be deemed necessary: correcting irregular or protruding teeth; restyling an unsatisfactory nose, chin, or ears; adding a hearing aid; reducing the signs of an aging face.

All these items, and more, will be discussed in the following chapters. But, first, let's consider why facial appearance has such importance in our lives.

Historically, attempts to gain insight into character through the study of appearance have ranged from superstition to reasoned thought—and from the sublime to the ridiculous. For example, Aristotle propounded a theory that humans resembled specific lesser animals and assumed some of the same characteristics as those animals.[2] This might be construed as the beginnings of physiognomy: the process of trying to judge character and mental ability by observation of physical features.

People are still, unknowingly, applying Aristotle's premise when they describe someone as looking like "a fox," "a weasel," "a pig"; "owlish" or "horsey." Frequently people are said to resemble their pets, especially cats and dogs. And Sir Winston Churchill's "bulldog look" was often linked to his tenacity during World War II.

A later idea of physiognomy held that facial expressions result from four basic emotions. The proponents of this idea said we are all ruled by one predominant emotion—melancholy, choler, phlegm, or sanguinity—and our characters are shaped accordingly. The stereotyped image of each character was said to be:

• *Melancholic:* gloomy, irritable, depressed, sad, sober, pensive.
• *Choleric:* quick-tempered, irascible, bilious.
• *Sanguine:* cheerful, confident, optimistic, hopeful, warm, passionate.
• *Phlegmatic:* dull, sluggish, apathetic, calm, cool, stolid.[3]

A different school of thought emerged in the late 1700s. Phrenology was based on the assumption (among others) that character and intelligence are determined by the size and shape of the head.

A final attempt to explain character combined some aspects of both physiognomy and phrenology. Based on Plato's three-part division of the human soul, this premise stated that humans are divided into three categories which correspond with specific facial shapes and types of features:

- *Mental:* "thinkers." Elongated or triangular-shaped faces.
- *Motor:* "doers." Square faces with sharp features.
- *Vital:* "sensualists." Round faces with flabby features.[4]

Amazingly, although we now know that facial shapes and features are determined by heredity, many of us still adhere to occasional stereotyped impressions of people based on the old principles of physiognomy and phrenology. To illustrate how some well-known people might have been judged by these character analysis methods, we've put together the photographs shown on pages 4–6 with a list of stereotyped personality descriptions based on facial features. Do you think these assessments are accurate?

According to the American Optometric Association, women in the United States have sometimes been judged by the color of their eyes. The color associations are gray—wise; black—mettlesome; green—needing tight control; blue—faithful; brown—"never let out of your sight."

More recently, an American psychologist and an English dentist advanced a theory that people whose faces are long and angular generally are practical, assertive, cheerful, and slightly naive, while those with short, square faces are apt to be shrewd, imaginative, dependent, and moody. They base this theory on work by researchers indicating that facial muscles can produce sufficient pressure to change the shape of bones during the time when the bones are maturing and are soft. Tension or relaxation of the muscles would, they speculate, result in "a short face and protrusion of the lower jaw" in inhibited, socially conforming people and longer faces in assertive people.[5]

WHAT DO WE REALLY KNOW?

Putting aside dubious theories about character assessment, what do we really know about the role appearance plays in our reactions to others and theirs to us?

When readers of *Glamour* magazine were asked to complete a brief survey on "The Impact of Beauty,"[6] they echoed many of the observations made by professional researchers. Some of their responses, along with sample quotations, were:

- Have you ever felt people wanted to get to know you or rejected you because of the way you look?

  92 percent: yes   4 percent: no   4 percent: not certain

Bulging forehead: quick-
tempered
(Tony Geary)

Heavy, arched eyebrows: dramatic
(Zubin Mehta)

"I've been rejected and even ostracized because of my physical
appearance. It seems that being overweight cancels five years of
college and fluency in four languages."
- Did you ever reject someone in a social situation because of his or
her physical appearance?
67 percent: yes   33 percent: no
"I am rather prejudiced against men who are not gorgeous and
women who don't wear makeup."

Drooping eyelids: suspicious
(Diane Keaton)

Close-set eyes: cunning
(Karen Black)

Protruding ears: clumsy
(Fred Astaire)

Tops of ears reaching above eyebrows: intelligent
(Raquel Welch)

- Do you think you ever gained a job or lost a job because of the
  way you look?
  56 percent: yes   32 percent: no   12 percent: not certain
- Do you think people respond to you more positively when you're
  wearing makeup and prettier clothes?
  94 percent: yes   3 percent: no   3 percent: not certain
  "When meeting people for the first time, their reactions usually
  depend on how I'm dressed and on my hair and makeup, rather

Thin, pointed nose: curious
(John Lennon)

Large earlobes: lucky
(Gloria Vanderbilt)

Wide mouth: generous
(Lena Horne)

Bulbous nose: insensitive
(W. C. Fields)

than on what I have to say."
• Do you feel that some of your colleagues at work are given special
  advantages because of their looks?
  45 percent: yes   37 percent: no   18 percent: not certain
  "I work for the federal government and it's amazing how the tall,
  slim, attractive people are assumed to be better at what they do than
  those who are shorter, plainer, or heavier."

Thin lips: stingy
(James Cagney)

Gap between front teeth:
pleasure-loving
(Sandra Day O'Connor)

- How do you view yourself?

  29 percent: very attractive   52 percent: fairly attractive

  17 percent: average   2 percent: unattractive

  "I feel that being nice-looking has actually closed doors for me. People think I need less than anyone else because I'm pretty."

- Do you think it's as important for a man to be attractive to succeed at work as for a woman?

  24 percent: yes   62 percent: no   14 percent: not certain

  "When a man is unattractive or unkempt at work, it's attributed to his being hard-working and under pressure, but an unattractive woman is thought to be lazy and sloppy and very uninteresting."

The role that appearance plays in social and professional judgments really shouldn't surprise us if we consider that an estimated 80 percent of our knowledge is acquired through visual impressions.[7] Add to that such influences of modern society as television, the burgeoning health and beauty industries, and increased competition for both men and women in the job market and it's easy to see why so many of us are seriously concerned with how we look. This concern has led increasing numbers of people, especially those in business, to actively seek ways of projecting the "right image" and creating a positive first impression.

Clinical research confirms that we do make snap judgments based on appearance—a fact that can be particularly hard on people who vary from the normal standards of attractiveness. Surely we can all remember situations in which we felt an immediate like or dislike for someone we had just met, even though we couldn't define *why* we were reacting that way. We just had a sense of "something that appeals to me" or "something that bothers me." Frequently, that "something" was an aspect of the other person's appearance, even if we didn't realize it. Since we generally don't have much time to get to know people during a first meeting, we come away with impressions based on superficial clues, among which their looks play a major part.

Why is appearance such an important factor in our personal and professional assessments? Social psychologists have recently begun to amass a substantive body of data on the relevance of attractiveness to our lives. One of the foremost researchers in this field is Dr. Ellen Berscheid, a professor at the University of Minnesota. Dr. Berscheid offers these comments related to first impressions: "Most people do not have their I.Q.'s tattooed on their foreheads, nor are their diplomas of educational accomplishment displayed prominently about their persons; an individual's financial status is a private matter between himself, his banker, and the Better Business Bureau; and we would not know how to interpret the structure of his genes even if he could present them to us for inspection."[8]

Therefore, we wind up with appearance as a gauge—and, rightly or wrongly, with Aristotle's observation that "Beauty is a greater recommendation than any letter of introduction," at least for first impressions.

Appearance is important to men as well as women. Professor Berscheid cites studies in which young men and women evaluated head and shoulder photographs of other people of varied degrees of attractiveness. They were asked to assess the individuals' personalities and guess about their personal and business lives. Says Dr. Berscheid: "Physically attractive people, as contrasted to the physically unattractive, were believed to be more sensitive, kind, interesting, strong, poised, modest, sociable, outgoing, exciting, and sexually warm and responsive persons. In addition, it was believed that attractive people will capture better jobs, have more successful marriages, and experience happier and more fulfilling lives than less attractive people."[9]

Dr. Gerald R. Adams, a professor of social psychology at Utah State University, points out that stereotyped images of a person's intelligence, ability, or other personal qualities that are derived from appearance have resulted in large numbers of our population being "stigmatized." Dr. Adams says: "For the attractive person, this stigma has positive attributional overtones. The message is that beauty implies goodness, talent, and success. Therefore, attractive people should be able to walk with their heads held high since everyone sees them in a socially desirable way. Also, when they are perceived as failing, this is construed merely as a case of stumbling but not falling. It is believed that attractive people will always get up again if they do go down. And if the unattractive person falls down, it is believed that [he is] not likely to get up again."[10]

What are some of the generally agreed-upon criteria for attractiveness? In a study of "The Judgment of Intelligence from Photographs",[11] Stuart W. Cook of the University of Minnesota reported the following common denominators among ten people photographed who were judged to have the highest intelligence:

1. Symmetry and regularity of features
2. Pleasantness of expression
3. Neatness of appearance

In terms of self-evaluation, satisfaction with specific physical characteristics has been found to influence a positive self-image. For men, the most important factors are complexion, nose, face, teeth, and hair texture (along with weight, waist, body build, and shape of thighs and legs); for women, the factors are complexion, face, profile, general appearance, eyes, chin, and hair color (along with weight distribution, waist, body build, thighs, chest, height, ankles, and hips).[12]

Of course, standards of attractiveness vary according to cultural and ethnic perceptions and trends; however, there are certain common denominators at any point in time. Although a fairly wide range of physical characteristics will meet accepted standards, any striking deviation often draws unwanted attention to the individual.

Sometimes people with less than classic features are compensated with exceptional ability or personality. For instance, Diana Vreeland, whose face might most kindly be described as "striking," rose to preeminence in the fashion world—probably one of the most appearance-conscious businesses in existence. In the same field, some people have succeeded despite "imperfect" features. Lauren Hutton turned the gap between her front teeth into an asset as a

Lauren Hutton

Diana Vreeland

model—and Brooke Shields and Margaux Hemingway have achieved top model status with dark and heavy eyebrows.

Or consider the large number of actors, singers, and dancers who have achieved high recognition—and, in some instances, set new standards for attractiveness—despite supposed flaws. Consider the following examples:

Brooke Shields

Margaux Hemingway

Bette Davis: wide mouth and pro-truding eyes (which inspired a hit song)

Barbra Streisand: prominent nose and teeth

Joan Crawford: wide mouth and heavy eyebrows

Robert Mitchum: drooping eye-lids

Martha Graham: prominent chin, mouth, and eyes

Kirk Douglas: deeply cleft chin

Carol Burnett: buck teeth and large mouth

Barry Manilow: prominent nose and eyes and heavy eyebrows

APPEARANCE AND THE WORKING WORLD

Despite its seeming importance, beauty isn't always a joy to the possessor, especially in the business world. In an article for *Working Woman* magazine, Elizabeth Wheeler writes: "It is possible that the extra bit of attention a pretty woman receives from almost all men—from top management to the janitor—is a help in her career. It also is possible that the resentment she can receive from peers, subordinates and anyone else who might think she is getting ahead because of what she looks like or whom she is sleeping with is a hindrance. And the latter, we are told, is more common than the former.

"Has life in the brave new world of the American corporation changed so little? It seems so. When we queried a group of high-powered women executives who happen to be pretty, their stories were similar. People make the same old assumptions about a beautiful woman, they reported, regardless of what she does for a living. Some will like her because she is attractive. Others mistrust her, perceiving her as a threat to their jobs and/or personal relationships. Still others will wonder, perhaps without meaning to be malicious or sexist, whether she's stupid, lazy or slept her way to her job."[13]

In the old double-standard tradition, researchers say that the same problems don't accrue to handsome men: ". . . men's character and personality will always shine through their appearance; both men and women look at them that way."[14]

An appearance factor that can be particularly detrimental is overweight. When the Maryland Commission on Human Rights studied the question of weight and size discrimination,[15] the research team reported "a clear pattern in that the obese are penalized by lower pay, inequitable hiring standards, relegation to non-contact public positions and other distinctive treatment, based on non-job related criteria." However, one of the employment agency representatives who was interviewed estimated that "overweight is 75 percent overlooked in males."

Among the examples of discrimination quoted in the report was the case of a legal secretary who was 50 pounds overweight. When she applied for a job, she was advised over the telephone that she seemed well-qualified. She told the researchers that, "As soon as I walked into the agency, the personnel executive began making all kinds of excuses like, 'I couldn't meet with the prospective employer.' I'm sure overweight was why I was turned away."

In another instance, a leading department store personnel executive told an applicant that there was no possibility of her being hired because, at 6′ 2″ and 300 pounds, she was overweight. "This woman was turned down by two nursing schools because she was overweight," the report says. "At one she was requested to lose 50 pounds; and when she succeeded, was asked to lose more weight and gave up. She was finally accepted at another nursing institution, completed her degree, was hired by a government agency. Her first evaluation said, 'You look unprofessional.'"

Employment agencies for positions in management and technical fields indicated that obese people were difficult to place in entry-level jobs in customer service and sales. However, if an overweight person had a good record in sales, he or she was placeable.

Another indication of the economic disadvantages of being overweight in a "thin is in" society comes from a survey[16] of 15,000 executives throughout the country. It revealed that of the executives earning $25,000 to $50,000 yearly, only nine percent were overweight; however, thirty-nine percent of the executives earning $10,000 to $20,000 were overweight. "Overweight" was defined as being more than ten pounds heavier than the standard insurance company weight chart maximum weight for a given height. The study was conducted by Robert Half, president of an international company specializing in financial and computer executive recruitment. Based on this and past surveys, Mr. Half estimates that "some fat people pay a penalty of $1,000 a pound" in the job market.

To make life even more difficult for today's career person, attractiveness is not the only stereotype used to judge appearance: youthful looks are also important for successful men and women. *Fortune* and *Working Woman* magazines both have devoted special coverage to the role of image in modern business circles. *Working Woman* contained these observations: "In business, the younger-looking candidate often is perceived as the better candidate. In order to compete successfully for promotions and jobs, some ambitious corporate professionals are resorting to 'defensive surgery' ('plastic' is passé). A tuck here and some fatty tissue removed from there can take ten to 15 years off a middle-aged face, male *or* female . . . . Women execs in their early 40s face two-fold competition: They must beat out younger women—as well as *all* men."[17]

That observation is borne out by a recent report from the National Commission on Working Women.[18] A study by the Commission revealed that older women seeking jobs do face the twofold discrimination of age and sex. "Women are classified as 'old' at an early age," the study contends. Furthermore, it cites a comment by an official of the Equal Employment Opportunity Commission: "One of the most common forms of employment discrimination against older women is the negative reverse of sexual harassment; the older woman excluded from a job opportunity because of a male selecting official, often young (but not necessarily so), acting upon his preference for young attractive women in positions under his supervision. This practice is widespread and occurs both in government and private industry." In spite of these handicaps, the study estimates that the number of working women between ages 45 and 54 will double during the next 20 years.

Overall, women of all ages comprise more than 43 percent of the work force. For them, as well as their male colleagues, the competition for first jobs and professional advancement is becoming much tougher, so they're all looking for ways to gain an advantage over the rest of the field.

Dr. Berscheid and sociologist Elaine Walster of the University of Wisconsin speculate that physical attractiveness is of greatest importance in "one-time-only" or "few-time" situations, such as job interviews and political campaigns. If this is true, they say, people whose jobs require primarily one-time-only interaction with others can be assumed to be most affected by physical-attractiveness stereotypes. Whereas, those whose work generally involves contact with the same group of people have the advantage of "familiarity" to balance the appearance factor.

The researchers comment: "One might go so far as to speculate that the apparent increase in the importance of physical attractiveness as evidenced by the proliferation of cosmetic . . . products, its emphasis in the media and in advertisements, is not only a result of our affluent society, but a consequence of the fact that we are all experiencing more one-time and few-time social contacts than ever before in the history of man. The invention of the television-telephone threatens to further attack the bastions of visual anonymity and to increase the influence of appearance."[19]

PROFESSIONAL HELP

In another presentation on this topic, Dr. Berscheid continues her comments on the theme of first impressions: "In a society in which one cannot even count on having the same set of parents for any length of time, the same marriage partner for any length of time, when one may be thrown into the dating and mating market at age 30, 40, 50, or even 60, when it becomes increasingly unlikely that one will have the same workmates, colleagues or neighbors for any length of time—in sum, in a society in which social fragmentation has proceeded to an unprecedented point . . . , people are constantly assessed very quickly by others simply on the basis of their appearance rather than upon their record of actual behavior and other characteristics. Is it any wonder, then, that to help them cope, people look to the new keepers of the fountain of beauty and youth—the dentists, the doctors, the plastic surgeons, the nutritionists, the cosmeticians, the physical therapists and so on?"[20]

In one of his papers on physical attractiveness, social psychologist Adams also acknowledges the increasing importance of the medical professional's role in matters of appearance: "Recognizing that physical attractiveness has powerful influences upon impressions *and* social behavior highlights the value of much which is accomplished by the field of medicine . . . assisting their patients beyond physical well-being. Assisting individuals toward positive physical appearance not only provides an appealing body image but also promotes positive socialization experiences which support healthy personality development."[21]

Another study reported by Dr. Berscheid illustrates how one medical area can influence judgments of appearance. It involved a group of women before and after cosmetic surgery. Controls included the stipulation that the women to be evaluated must be within the normal range of appearance prior to surgery and that post-operative photographs appear to be regular snapshots. The results indicated that the "cosmetic surgery actually increased the physical attractiveness level of the individuals who were depicted in the photos." Dr. Berscheid found that raters viewed the women as "more competent marriage partners and more likely to marry the person of their choice after surgery than before surgery. Further, there was a significant change in their perceived social and professional happiness after surgery. Finally, each rater's estimate of how much they would personally *like* the individual, how much they *would like working* with them on some task, and how much they would actually *like to meet* with them changed significantly, in a positive direction. This study suggests, then, that cosmetic surgery patients, even those whose state before surgery is not anywhere near the unattractive end of the continuum, ought to start receiving concrete social benefits from their improved physical appearance immediately following surgery."[22]

My own years of experience in reconstructive and cosmetic surgery indicate both a high degree of satisfaction with the results and positive changes in patients' lives. Frequently, patients begin to make other changes in their appearance once the surgery is completed—experimenting with new hairstyles, clothing and cosmetics. I have also observed that they tend to become more confident, to feel less anxious and awkward in social situations, and to welcome opportunities for greater visibility in professional, community, or social organizations.

Similar reactions have been observed by experts in other appearance-related fields. All the specialists who shared their professional expertise with me for this book related examples of patients or clients for whom both major and minor improvements in appearance resulted in tangible benefits.

A study conducted for Clairol by Dr. Judith Waters, a psychology professor at Fairleigh Dickinson University, produced "dollars and cents" evidence that an attractive appearance counts in the job market.[23] Potential employers were shown photographs of women as they normally appeared or after their hair had been styled and colored and their makeup changed. No drastic changes were made and no theatrical makeup was used. Clothing and facial expressions were the same in both photographs. A before or after photograph was attached to résumés detailing various job-related skills. None of the personnel managers in the study saw both a before and after photograph of the same woman.

The personnel directors were asked to rate each job applicant and estimate how much she could expect to earn. The results Dr. Waters reported were:

1. Physical appearance does indeed play an important role in the hiring process, particularly at entry/reentry skill levels.
2. Increases in before and after mean salaries were found ranging between 8 percent and 20 percent on base salaries of $10,500–12,100.
3. That appearance is taken into account was indicated even by the comments made by the personnel directors. Examples are:
   "Doesn't look like an organized person. Should pull herself together."
   "Not very neat. I wouldn't hire her, even though it seems like she is qualified in what she has done."
   "Appearance is fine, looks very business-oriented—looks efficient."
   "Just what you want a good secretary to look like."

Additional comments related specifically to professional image included:

"Excellent appearance—corporate image."

"If someone came in looking like this, I couldn't send them out. Would be surprised if she was with [Company X]—that's not their look."

"She looks like she'd have to stay in a non-profit type organization. Doesn't seem to have corporate business image."

"Her hair is messy—image is important to us."

People in the political arena are also becoming more concerned about their appearance according to writer Karen Feld. In researching an article for *TV Guide* on political figures who have had cosmetic surgery, Ms. Feld found increasing activity in this area.

She learned that a number of politicians have had hair transplants, including Senator Strom Thurmond. In referring to his young wife and children, Senator Thurmond told Ms. Feld that he felt he had the energy of a younger man and that looking younger helped to make him feel younger. Another politician who has had a hair transplant is Senator Joe Biden, a presidential hopeful in his thirties who was concerned that he appeared older because of premature balding. Among the other politicians who have had hair transplants are Congressmen Andy Jacobs and Tom Railsback and Governor Charles Thone.

Senator Henry "Scoop" Jackson and Congressmen Barry M. Goldwater, Jr. and Sonny Montgomery are among the political figures who have had eye-lift surgery—the most popular cosmetic procedure for men.

Ms. Feld suggests that heightened visibility is one of the reasons politicians are seeking surgical and other image-enhancing options. Rapid transportation carries politicians to every part of the country. Furthermore, the influx of television news programs regularly brings them into the homes of their constituents, making politicians subject to closer public scrutiny than at any previous period in history.

Politicians aren't alone in the electronic jungle. Technology already has begun influencing decisions others make about many of us. Companies such as Xerox, International Business Machines (IBM), and Union Carbide now review certain potential employees on videotape to determine which ones will be given personal job interviews. And this trend is expected to become even more prevalent in the coming years.

For this reason, and others previously cited, we must all pay greater attention to our appearance. The information that follows can help you improve your chance of creating the "right" first impression by becoming your own image specialist.

Everyone wants to make the right first impression. Helping *you* do that is what this book is about. The possibilities for enhancing your image are numerous and varied. Since clothing hides or camouflages most of our bodies, our faces are the areas subjected to the closest scrutiny. Therefore, the "how-to" information and guidelines in this book concentrate on the face and what most greatly influences its appearance.

I'll tell you everything you need to know in order to improve the face you present to your personal and professional associates. I will cover in detail the many factors involved in facial appearance and suggest how you can "put your best face forward."

2

ANALYZING YOUR IMAGE

"I wear my face from right to left.
You see it left to right.
A mirror image, quite reversed,
Projects upon your sight."[24]

Are you really aware of your mirror image? Of what you project to others? How well do you know "that other self"—the you who, consciously or subconsciously, creates the public image?

Do you really know what you'd like your image to be? If you haven't really thought about how you want others to see you, this is the time to assess what's important to your professional and/or personal success.

First, how do you define success in terms of your current goals?
Professional: getting a first job, advancement within your present company, a move to a new company, a complete career change, increased professional recognition, greater responsibility, larger income.
Personal: an improved social life, a new or improved personal relationship, marriage, increased recognition in your community, greater involvement in community activities.

What are the most important elements necessary for achieving each goal? Over which of these factors do you have some measure of control? Are you prepared to act on those items? Would any changes in your appearance be beneficial in reaching your goals? Are these changes you can and would be willing to make?

Now consider image. How would you like to be regarded by your business associates? By your family and friends? How are you regarded now? Select a role model—someone you consider successful, personally or professionally.

1. What image does this person convey?
2. What aspects of his or her appearance contribute to this image?
3. What qualities of character or professional conduct contribute to the image?
4. What similarities are there between you and your role model?
5. In what ways are you different?
6. What about this person would you most like to emulate?
7. Can you realistically expect to acquire the desired characteristics and, if so, what steps must you take to do so? Are you willing to take them?
8. In what ways is your appearance related to creating this image?

Meeting new people, job-hunting, preparing for a career change or promotion—all these are essentially "selling" situations. We place our talents, ideas, and personalities on the market, hoping to attract others to us. Because our appearance does influence those important first-impression responses we elicit from others, in professional as well as social situations, we need to know whether our appearance suits the image we want to project.

Before selling your house, the first step is to have it appraised: determine the assets and liabilities, decide what improvements are necessary to increase its value. You shouldn't do less for yourself than you'd do for your house. Why not make an appointment with yourself for a realistic self-appraisal of how to best "sell" yourself?

Allot a quiet block of time with no outside distractions. Realize that you're the best judge of how you look and feel—when you're completely honest with yourself. This means noting your good points, as well as the areas that could use improvement.

The lists of questions in this chapter are designed to help you assess your present image, as well as the image you'd like to present to the world. To begin, take a close look at pictures of yourself. If you don't have any that show both sides of your profile, as well as the back of your head, ask a family member or friend to photograph you from these angles. Study your facial shape, eye and eyebrow shape, length of jaw, width of nose, shape and size of ears, and angle of chin. Look closely at your face in the mirror and feel your cheekbones, browbones, temples, and chin. Become totally familiar with the structure of your face.

Now, how do you honestly feel about your facial appearance? Is there some aspect that makes you uncomfortable or self-conscious—and is this creating problems in your dealings with other people? Do you believe that supposed signs of aging make you appear older than you feel or are?

Consider these points as you answer the following questions. (Each topic will be treated in later chapters, as noted.)

HEAD, FACE, AND SKIN (Treated in Chapters 3 and 4)

- What is the size of your head (large, average, small)?
- How does your head look from the back?
- What is the basic shape of your face (see illustrations pages 22–24)?
- Is your face fat, normal, thin?
- What is the dominant shade of your skin? What are the underlying tones?
- What is the texture of your skin (coarse, normal, fine)?
- Is your skin normal, oily, dry, or combination (see page 34)?
- What is the tone of your facial skin (firm, beginning to sag, slack)?
- How does your skin feel to the touch?
- How is your complexion?
- Is your skin flaky or scaly?
- Do you have enlarged pores? Small pores?

Oval

Balanced proportions with width about three-fourths the length.

Round

Chin and hairline are rounded; length and width are similar in proportions.

Square

Angular features with a wide jaw line and forehead.

Rectangle

Length of face is proportionately greater in respect to width than other shapes.

- Do you have acne or other scars, blackheads, whiteheads, moles, blemishes, or birthmarks?
- In the sun, do you tan easily or burn?
- If you wear foundation makeup or bronzer, does it look natural?
- When did you last change the color of your foundation or bronzer?
- Does your makeup or bronzer look fresh and natural?
- What is the overall effect of your facial appearance, both full face and in profile?

Diamond

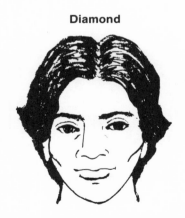

Forehead is narrow and chin is small or pointed; greatest width is across the cheek bones.

Pear

Wide jaw line, full cheeks, and narrower forehead.

Heart

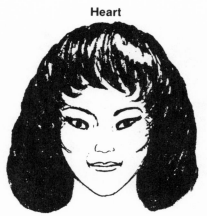

Forehead is wide; chin is narrow
and pointed.

HAIR (Treated in Chapter 5)

- What dominant color is your hair? What highlight shades does it have?
- Is your hair turning gray?
- If you color your hair, how long have you worn your present shade?
- What is the length of your hair?
- How is your hair styled?
- How does your hairstyle look from the back and sides?
- How long have you worn your present hair length and style?
- What characterizes your hair (fine, coarse, thick, thin, curly, straight, oily, dry)?
- Do you have dandruff or other scalp problems?
- Is your hairline scraggly or receding?
- Do you wear a wig or hairpiece?
- Do you generally wear a hat?

FOREHEAD, EYEBROWS, AND EYES (Treated in Chapter 6)

- Do you have lines or wrinkles on your forehead/brow area or around your eyes?
- Is your forehead high, average, or low?
- What color are your eyebrows and eyelashes?
- What is the shape of your eyebrows (arched, curved, straight, slanted)?

24

- Do your eyebrows grow together?
- Are your eyebrows heavy, average or sparse?
- What is the shape of your eyes (see illustrations below)?
- What color are your eyes?
- Do your eyelids sag?
- Do you have discoloration beneath your eyes?
- Do your eyes look bloodshot?
- Do you squint?
- Do you have vision problems?
- If you wear eyeglasses, describe the frames.
- When was the last time you changed the style?
- Do you wear contact lenses?
- For women, what types of eye makeup do you generally use and what effect does it create?
- For women, what color combinations of eye makeup do you generally use and when did you last make a major change in colors?
- Do you use concealing makeup under your eyes?
- Do you look at people when you're talking to them?

Small Eyes/Small Lids

Large Eyes/Small Lids

Small Eyes/Prominent Lids

Large Eyes/Prominent Lids

Oriental Eyes

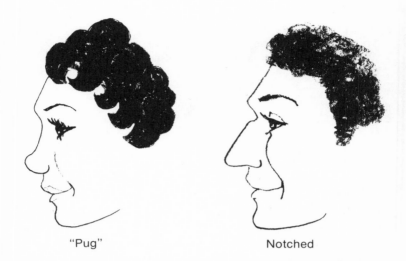

"Pug"   Notched

NOSE, CHEEKS, AND EARS (Treated in Chapter 7)

- What size and shape is your nose (see illustrations pages 26–27)?
- How does your nose look in profile? Full face?
- Does your nose balance your other features (see page 160)?
- Do you have difficulty breathing through your nose?
- Do you have broken veins around your nose?
- Is your nose discolored?
- What is the placement of your cheekbones (high, average, low)?
- What is the shape of your cheeks (rounded, smooth, sunken)?

Ski   Open Nostril

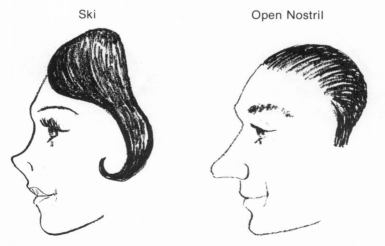

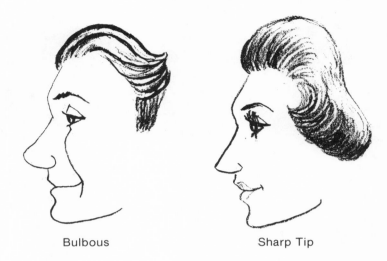

Bulbous   Sharp Tip

- For women, do you contour your cheeks?
- For women, do you have unwanted hair on your cheeks?
- What size and shape are your ears (see illustration page 28)?
- Do your ears protrude from or lie flat against your head?
- Do you have hearing problems?
- Do you wear a hearing aid (if so, what kind)?
- For women, are your ears pierced?
- For women, what style earrings do you generally wear?

Blunt Tip   Hooked

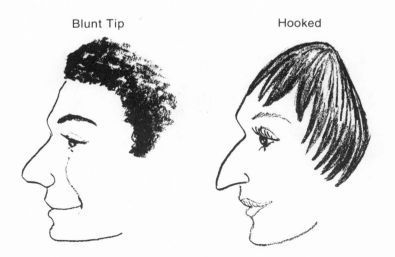

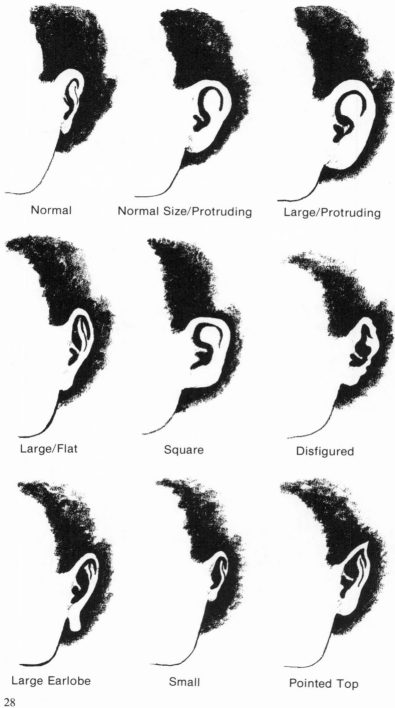

Normal   Normal Size/Protruding   Large/Protruding

Large/Flat   Square   Disfigured

Large Earlobe   Small   Pointed Top

MOUTH, TEETH, CHIN, AND NECK (Treated in Chapters 8 and 9)

- What size and shape is your mouth (see illustrations pages 29–30)?
- For women, do you have unwanted hair around your mouth?
- Do you have lines around your mouth?
- For women, what lipstick colors do you generally wear and when did you last make a major change in colors?
- What do your teeth look like (straight, uneven, small, large, white, stained, gapping, chipped)?
- Do you try to conceal your teeth when you smile?
- Do you have problems with your teeth?
- Do your jaws fit together properly or do your upper or lower teeth protrude?
- What does your chin look like (small, medium, large, strong, weak, dimpled)?
- In profile, does your chin balance your other features (see page 188)?
- How is your chin line (firm, some sagging, jowls/double/triple chins)?
- For men, if you have a beard, what is the shape and how long have you worn this shape?
- Is it neatly clipped?
- For men, if you have a moustache, what is the shape and how long have you worn this shape?
- Is it neatly clipped?
- For men, if you have a beard or moustache, does the color match the hair on your head?

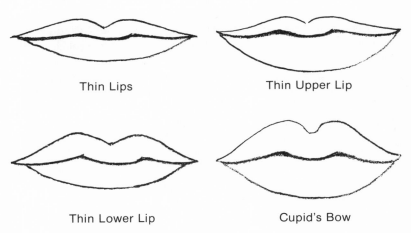

Thin Lips   Thin Upper Lip

Thin Lower Lip   Cupid's Bow

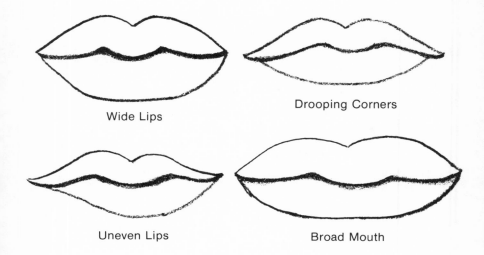

Wide Lips

Drooping Corners

Uneven Lips

Broad Mouth

- What colors do you generally wear closest to your face?
- What type of neckline or collar/lapel style do you generally wear?
- For men, what width tie do you generally wear? What size knot do you use?
- For women, what kind of jewelry or other accessories do you generally wear around your neck?
- Do you hold your chin and neck erect?

Now that you've taken a closer look at your facial appearance, what kind of image do you think you're projecting? Is it the one you want to convey? Is there room for improvement?

If you believe that changing any aspect of your facial appearance might contribute to a more successful image, read on. The following chapters offer guidelines for and information on a vast array of options for facial improvements—from do-it-yourself projects to professional assistance from medical and other specialists. Each chapter concentrates on a specific area of the face or on an important factor related to facial appearance. In the final chapter, you will find suggestions for locating the right experts to help you.

3
NATURE'S PACKAGING

"Is it one of my well-looking days, child? Am I in face today?"[25]

As a plastic surgeon, I'm literally faced with the results of years of improper skin treatment. While age, weather, lifestyle, and environment eventually take their toll on all of us, many of the conditions people hope to correct with plastic surgery can be avoided or at least postponed through patience and lifelong care.

There are many popular myths surrounding care of the skin, most often with regard to wrinkling:

Myth 1: Facial masks will prevent or rid the skin of wrinkles.

The only way to remove wrinkles is plastic surgery. Masks make the skin feel "tighter" and "plump up" wrinkles temporarily with added moisture but have no lasting effect.

Myth 2: Oils and emollients will "nourish," "refine," or "restore" skin.

Skin is fed from inside the body by a diet incorporating healthy foods and plenty of water. Externally applied oils or emollients provide no nourishment. Moisturizers do have a purpose—to help seal in natural moisture and oils—but do not "restore" or "refine" the skin.

Myth 3: Adults don't have to worry about acne.

Because you never had acne as a teenager, or had it and got rid of it, doesn't mean you'll never have to deal with the problem as an adult. Acne results from the clogging of pores by excess oil. The oil-producing glands in your skin react to hormones—and these are determined by heredity. So if your parents had acne, you probably will too, and the condition may recur all through life. Keeping skin clean and free of excess oil will help, but if you're troubled with acne, you'll need to treat it. Ignoring the problem won't make it go away.

Myth 4: Long hours in the sun won't damage skin.
There's much concern today with the increase in skin cancer, dark spots, wrinkles, and skin damage because of overexposure to sunlight. If you must be in the sun for long periods, you should protect yourself from overexposure.

Myth 5: Alcohol and tobacco don't affect skin appearance.
There is reliable evidence that smoking and excessive drinking *do* affect the appearance and texture of skin. Smoking and alcohol are general health hazards, robbing the skin of vital nutrients, moisture, and oxygen.

Myth 6: Crash diets don't affect the skin.
Too rapid weight loss, especially when unaccompanied by a regular exercise program, may result in stretching and sagging skin.

Myth 7: Skin care regimens should never vary.
Skin has a tendency to dry with advancing age, so you'll periodically need to reassess your skin care regimen. The activities you enjoy, the environment in which you live, the amount of sleep you get—every aspect of your lifestyle—also affect the condition of your skin. These, too, should be considered and adjustments to your skin care program made accordingly.

Myth 8: Pores "shrink" or "steam open."
Finally, the idea that pores open, close, or shrink at the drop of a hat is a figment of the imagination. Pores are openings in the skin surface for oil glands, hair follicles, and sweat glands. They may appear to close when the skin around them swells; they will appear enlarged by blackheads or may indeed enlarge as an oil gland enlarges. Their size, however, cannot be cosmetically altered. You can cover them with makeup, and keeping them free of blackheads or pimples will make them less noticeable. But don't be fooled by products that claim to shrink or open them.

SKIN STRUCTURE AND TYPES

To understand the basics of skin care, you should know some general facts about skin structure. Besides presenting the individual characteristics of appearance, skin is quite a marvelous organ—the largest of the body. It covers and protects all the other organs from

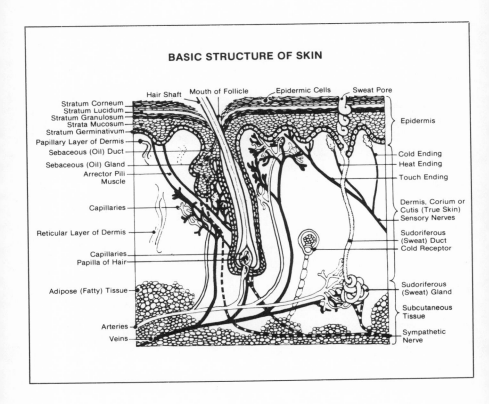

BASIC STRUCTURE OF SKIN

Hair Shaft — Mouth of Follicle — Epidermic Cells — Sweat Pore

Stratum Corneum
Stratum Lucidum
Stratum Granulosum
Strata Mucosum
Stratum Germinativum
Papillary Layer of Dermis
Sebaceous (Oil) Duct
Sebaceous (Oil) Gland
Arrector Pili Muscle
Capillaries
Reticular Layer of Dermis
Capillaries
Papilla of Hair
Adipose (Fatty) Tissue
Arteries
Veins

Epidermis
Cold Ending
Heat Ending
Touch Ending
Dermis, Corium or Cutis (True Skin)
Sensory Nerves
Sudoriferous (Sweat) Duct
Cold Receptor
Sudoriferous (Sweat) Gland
Subcutaneous Tissue
Sympathetic Nerve

bacteria, sun, moisture loss, and harmful chemicals in the air. It keeps your body at the right temperature through the sweat glands, eliminates toxic wastes, and gives your tactile senses a means of perceiving the world around you.

The skin is made up of many layers, varying in thickness from very thin and delicate around the eyes to as much as one-half inch thick on your palms. The two outer layers, epidermis and dermis, are most important for our purposes.

The outer layer, or epidermis, consists of many layers of a protein-like substance called keratin. Under the epidermis lies the dermis, the most active layer of the skin. These two layers function as a team—the epidermis providing fresh, new cells that work their way up to the surface every 15 days or so; the dermis nurturing the epidermis with blood and holding the sweat glands, hair follicles, oil glands, and nerve tissue. The dermis also carries the genetic influences of oil production, acne, and sensitivity to sunlight.

Collagen, a fibrous protein that makes up 90 percent of our skin, provides elasticity and suppleness and helps retain moisture in the skin. When collagen breaks down through prolonged overexposure to the sun or the aging process, skin loses its firmness, becomes dry, and begins to wrinkle.

Skin color is determined by the amount of melanin (pigmentation that protects the skin from ultraviolet rays) it contains. Black skin, which comes in more than 30 shades, has the greatest concentration of melanin. Oriental skin is in the middle range, and Caucasian skin, with a range of about 10 skin tones, contains the smallest quantity of melanin.

Both men and women are born with the same types of skin, which fall into one of four basic types: oily, dry, normal, or combination. The characteristics of each skin type are:

- *Oily skin* produces excess sebum (an oily lubricant) which makes it the perfect environment for acne, pimples, blackheads, and other blemishes. In appearance it is thick, irregular, and shiny and has distended pores. One advantage of oily skin is that it's usually the last skin type to show the typical signs of aging. Some clues for determining whether you have oily skin are: makeup color fades away after several hours; a tissue becomes translucent when blotted on your nose or cheeks; your skin looks shiny after a few hours; you tan easily without tending to burn.
- *Dry skin* occurs when too much moisture escapes from the epidermis and not enough is replaced by the dermis. In appearance it has a fine, regular, transparent texture with very small pores and fine superficial wrinkles. Dry skin flakes easily and is especially susceptible to the effects of sun, wind, dry heat, air conditioning, and pollution. Some clues for determining whether you have dry skin are: you sunburn easily; your skin flakes easily; when washed with soap, your skin feels tight.
- *Normal skin* is a rare treasure—neither too oily nor too dry. In appearance it has a smooth texture, is blemish-free, and has no enlarged pores.
- *Combination skin* generally has the characteristics of an oily skin in the "T-zone" (forehead, nose, and chin) and dry skin on the cheeks and around the eyes.

If you're unsure about your skin type, an expert esthetician (a trained skin care specialist) can help you—and the cost of an analysis isn't expensive. Kay Acuazzo, president of the Skin Care Association of America and co-owner of Paul & Kay's Beauty Villa in Philadelphia, says many women and men come to her thinking they have dry skin, only to discover that it is, in fact, oily. "Just because your skin is flaking doesn't mean it's dry," she explains. "You can flake from bacteria within the skin. You may have asphyxiated skin that is oily underneath but dry on top. In this case you want to alleviate the surface dryness while treating the oiliness underneath."

COMBATING THE AGING PROCESS

The condition of our skin changes as we age. Because it's so much finer than that on other parts of our bodies, our facial skin is especially susceptible to the aging process. The condition of our skin changes, becoming drier because of decreased sebum production. Reduced elasticity results in sagging eyelid, cheek, chin, and neck skin and wrinkling on the forehead and around our eyes and mouth. Because their thicker skin and beards help retard wrinkling, men are better protected than women.

The most basic elements for combating the aging process, acne and other skin problems are diet, water, exercise, sleep, and a regimen of cleaning/moisturizing/protecting. These are the key ingredients to maintaining a youthful appearance and healthy skin.

A look at Jacqueline Onassis, Jane Fonda, Alan Alda, Lena Horne, Audrey Hepburn, John Forsythe, Faye Dunaway, Dinah Shore, Paul Newman, Rita Moreno and a long list of other well-known "over 40s" is a testimonial to ongoing skin and body care programs. So let's consider more closely the elements involved.

Diet

A well-balanced diet is essential to healthy skin (and hair). This means providing essential nutrients, vitamins, and minerals by eating foods rich in complex carbohydrates and protein, low in refined sugars and elements such as caffeine, and with reduced amounts of saturated fats (as found in animal products like meat, eggs, milk, and cheese and in vegetable shortening, lard, and palm oil).

THE MAJOR NUTRIENTS[26]

MAJOR NUTRIENTS	PRIMARY FUNCTIONS	SOURCES
Protein (should comprise 12 percent of total daily calories)	*Build and maintain health and vitality of skin, hair, and all body tissues *Help resist infections and protect against many degenerative conditions *Supply energy if diet has inadequate fats and carbohydrates	Best: fish, poultry, meat, eggs, milk, cheese Good: nuts, legumes, lentils, peanut butter
Carbohydrates (starches and naturally occurring sugars should comprise 48–58 percent of total daily calories; refined and processed sugars, 0–10 percent; total carbohydrate should be 58 percent of diet)	*Supply energy *Provide roughage or bulk (fiber) *Spare protein for body building and maintenance	Starches: grain products (cereals, breads, pasta, rice); many vegetables (particularly potatoes, peas, corn, beans) Fiber: whole grain foods, fruits, vegetables—also supply nutrients Sugars: honey, molasses, jam, jelly, syrups, all forms of sugar—supply few, if any, nutrients
Fats (should comprise 30 percent of total daily calories, divided equally between saturated, polyunsaturated, and monounsaturated fats; cholesterol intake limited to 300 mg. maximum)	*Supply concentrated source of calories *Help keep skin smooth and healthy *Carry fat-soluable vitamins (A, D, E, K)	Butter, margarine, oils, cream, dairy products made from whole milk, nuts, meats, poultry, egg yolks
Vitamin A	*Helps keep skin smooth and healthy *Helps body resist infections *Helps eyes adjust to changing conditions of light and dark (especially important in night driving) *Important for keeping all body tissues strong and healthy	Dark green leafy vegetables, orange and deep yellow fruits and vegetables, tomatoes, watermelon, dairy products fortified with vitamin A, eggs, liver

36

Nutrient	Functions	Food Sources
B-Vitamins	*Essential for releasing food energy and using protein to build and maintain tissues *Keep skin, nerves, and digestive system healthy	Meats, fish, poultry, organ meats, enriched or whole-grain breads and cereals, milk, cheese, eggs, nuts, legumes, green leafy vegetables
Vitamin C	*Helps keep tissues such as skin, blood vessels, gums, and muscles strong and healthy *Important in resisting infection and healing injured tissues	Citrus fruits, tomatoes, strawberries, green peppers, broccoli, leafy greens, white potatoes, cantaloupe
Vitamin D	*Necessary for body to properly use calcium and phosphorus (both essential for strong bones and teeth)	Dairy products fortified with vitamin D, fish, liver oils, sunshine (!)
Vitamin E	*Appears to retard breakdown of cell membranes and vitamin A (functions in human body are not fully understood)	Green leafy vegetables, whole grain products, vegetable oils, liver, meat, eggs, milk
Vitamin K	*Necessary for blood clotting	Green leafy vegetables (also produced by bacteria in intestinal tract, so this vitamin is not usually a problem unless bacteria have been reduced by drugs such as antibiotics)
Minerals	*Overall: combine with other nutrients to become part of the structure of many parts of the body (for example: calcium and phosphorus become part of bone tissue; iron becomes part of hemoglobin) *Become part of the regulatory systems that control such processes as energy use, muscle action, digestion, use of other nutrients, blood clotting, respiration, and fluid balance in body and nervous system	Dairy products, fruits and vegetables, nuts, grain products, meat, fish, poultry, legumes

The best skin care products can't make up for a lack of sufficient and effective nourishment. Nutritional imbalance may contribute to many common skin problems.

Obviously diet also is related to weight gain and loss. Extreme overweight may give the face a bloated appearance, while underweight can produce a gaunt look—neither of which is attractive to most people. Fad diets provide severely limited supplies of certain nutrients and/or cause too rapid weight gain or loss. This can upset the delicate balance of your entire body, including your skin. In addition to the havoc that can be wrought to the nourishment of your skin, rapid weight gain or loss strains the skin's natural elasticity and can result in sagging.

Underweight can be as dangerous as overweight; in fact, recent studies indicate that underweight people have a higher mortality rate than the obese. Two serious medical conditions are associated with underweight—bulimarexia, a syndrome of binge eating followed by purging (self-induced vomiting or large laxative intake); and anorexia nervosa, in which fear of weight gain causes people (especially young women) to quite literally starve themselves, sometimes to the point of death.

As in other areas of our lives, weight control is best handled without extreme measures. In one of my previous books, I provided guidelines for a varied, balanced eating program that can be adapted to fit individual tastes and lifestyles. The table shown here gives the recommended daily servings of major nutrients, their primary functions, and good sources.

Water

Not only is it essential to life, water is the single most important element in nutrition. Without it, the body couldn't utilize the nutrients from the foods we eat. Water is vital for maintaining healthy skin cells as well as eliminating wastes and regulating body temperature (two of the benefits of perspiration).

Moisture accounts for 50 to 75 percent of your skin's composition and it can only come from within. Moisturizers (see page 46) are actually products designed to help your skin retain its natural water supply. Keeping the moisture in is especially important in the winter when cold, drying winds can deplete the skin's moisture level and also in very hot, dry climates, which also sap moisture from the skin.

To maintain the skin's moisture supply, I recommend drinking two to three quarts of water each day in addition to the water you get from foods and beverages. If you're unaccustomed to this amount of fluid intake, your kidneys will need a few weeks to adjust. Also, if you participate regularly in strenuous exercise, you'll need to replenish the estimated three to five quarts of water that can be lost through prolonged physical exertion. As with any other good thing, you can get too much water, which will result in bloating. Two or three quarts a day is ample for most people.

Exercise

A good general workout gives skin the healthy, natural glow that no makeup can imitate. This is because exercise nourishes the skin by increasing blood circulation, which is the body's means of supplying oxygen to and removing impurities from the skin. The chart on page 40 summarizes a survey by the President's Council on Physical Fitness, rating the benefits of various popular forms of exercise.

Recent scientific studies conducted with athletes indicate that regular vigorous exercise may help replenish the skin's collagen content, contributing to the skin's thickness, strength, and elasticity. Research by exercise physiologist Dr. James White, coordinator of physical fitness at the University of California at San Diego, compared a group of older women engaged in a regular exercise program

RATINGS OF VARIOUS FORMS OF EXERCISE

This chart summarizes how seven fitness experts working with the President's Council on Physical Fitness rated some of the most popular sports and exercises. Ratings are on a scale of 0 to 3; thus a rating of 21 indicates maximum benefit (a score of 3 by all seven panelists). Ratings were made on the basis of regular (minimum of four times per week), vigorous (duration of 30 minutes to 1 hour per session) participation in each activity.

	Jogging	Bicycling	Swimming	Skating (Ice or Roller)	Handball/Squash	Skiing—Nordic	Skiing—Alpine	Basketball	Tennis	Calisthenics	Walking	Golf*	Softball	Bowling
PHYSICAL FITNESS														
Cardiorespiratory endurance (stamina)	21	19	21	18	19	19	16	19	16	10	13	8	6	5
Muscular endurance	20	18	20	17	18	19	18	17	16	13	14	8	8	5
Muscular strength	17	16	14	15	15	15	15	15	14	16	11	9	7	5
Flexibility	9	9	15	13	16	14	14	13	14	19	7	8	9	7
Balance	17	18	12	20	17	16	21	16	16	15	8	8	7	6
GENERAL WELL-BEING														
Weight control	21	20	15	17	19	17	15	19	16	12	13	6	7	5
Muscle definition	14	15	14	14	11	12	14	13	13	18	11	6	5	5
Digestion	13	12	13	11	13	12	9	10	12	11	11	7	8	7
Sleep	16	15	16	15	12	15	12	12	11	12	14	6	7	6
TOTAL	148	142	140	140	140	139	134	134	128	126	102	66*	64	51

*Ratings for golf are based on the fact that many Americans use a golf cart and/or caddy. If you walk the links, the physical fitness value moves up appreciably.

with a group that was sedentary. The findings were that the exercise group looked younger, had fewer wrinkles, and had better skin color. Bags under the eyes also tended to disappear following exercise.

As I observed in my fitness and nutrition book: "The way you structure your personal exercise program will depend on your age, physical condition, and lifestyle. However, some form of aerobic exercise is generally considered essential to the effectiveness of any exercise plan. Running or jogging, rapid walking, rope jumping, swimming, bicycling, skating, cross-country skiing, rowing, and aerobic dance are among the best and most popular forms of aerobic exercise. All contribute to the strength and development of your cardiovascular system and your body's ability to utilize oxygen efficiently.[27] Such exercises are important for general well-being as well as for healthy skin.

Whatever aerobic activities you choose for your exercise plan, the exercise should meet the following criteria:
• Be vigorous enough to tax your muscle strength
• Continue long enough and be strenuous enough to produce a feeling of healthy fatigue
• Involve the muscles and joints in many parts of your body
• Be done for at least 30 minutes at least three times a week

The following suggestions may be useful in selecting and sticking with an exercise program that will work for you.
1. First, get a check-up to determine your general condition and any specific medical considerations that may influence your decisions.
2. Consider your lifestyle and try to realistically assess when and how you can insert a regular exercise program into your normal routine. For instance, if you're an early riser, you might comfortably insert exercise into your pre-work schedule. However, if you like to sleep until the last possible moment, a lunch-time or evening workout may be your best choice.
3. Decide how much time you're willing to invest in exercise each week. Although you'll receive the same aerobic benefits whether you briskly walk or jog two miles, the latter will require about one-half to one-third less time.
4. Evaluate the conditions under which you're most likely to stick with your exercise regimen. Do you need the social stimulation and interaction of an activity such as tennis, basketball, raquetball, aerobic dancing, or roller skating with a partner? Or, would you prefer exercise (like walking, bicycling, jogging, or lap swimming) that provides an opportunity for solitude and an escape from competition?
5. Decide what you want to accomplish—general toning up, weight loss, cardiovascular benefits. Then, set realistic goals and a time frame for accomplishing them.
6. Start slowly and don't try to do too much, too soon. Gradually increasing your activity level is safer than overexerting yourself when your body hasn't been properly prepared. Also, overdoing often leads to muscle strain, which may discourage you from continuing to exercise.
7. Always warm up before and cool down after each exercise session with a series of simple stretching and bending exercises.
8. Try to stick with your weekly goals, even though this may be difficult in the beginning. Establishing any new habit takes time.

9. If you become tired or winded, slow down or stop for a while. Your energy level will be greater on some days than on others. Pay attention to your body's messages.
10. If you feel ill or experience pain while exercising, stop. These are your body's warning signals that something's wrong.
11. Don't compare your progress to anyone else's. You aren't in competition.
12. Periodically reassess your exercise program and make any necessary adjustments.

A special word about facial exercises: Various forms of facial exercises are currently popular. As both a plastic surgeon and ear-nose-throat surgeon, I have an intimate knowledge of every aspect of the human head and neck. I have found that devotees of facial exercise aren't properly informed about the interrelationship between the skin and the muscles of the face. The 30 parchment-thin facial muscles, which can produce more than 250,000 expressions, are the only muscles directly attached to the skin. Because of this, any movement of these muscles moves the attached facial skin. Facial exercises can make the skin less able to spring back due to the loss of elastic fibers (collagen). The result, in conjunction with the normal aging process, is wrinkling and sagging skin.

With age, there is also an accumulation of fatty deposits under the chin, causing a "double chin." A predisposition to this condition is largely hereditary. Double chins are affected by but are not entirely based on weight; even thin people can acquire a double chin as they grow older. Because this is a problem of fat accumulation and is totally unrelated to muscles of any kind, those who are not predisposed to these fatty deposits through heredity can best control the problem through diet rather than exercise.[28]

Sleep

Rest and relaxation can definitely affect how you look. Ironically, overexertion is rarely the cause of sleeplessness. Stress is one of the chief culprits of the bleary eyes, dark circles, and tension lines I see every day in my office. Illness and poor nutrition are other major factors.

Whatever the reasons, at one time or another, we've all experienced the debilitating effects of sleeplessness: red, puffy eyelids; weakness; irritability; and inability to concentrate or focus on simple tasks. While the realm of sleep and dreams is still vastly unexplored, we do know that constant lack of sleep is a serious threat to physical health, mental stability—and appearance.

We seem to achieve the best sleep of our lives at about 15 years of age, and many of us spend our ensuing years trying to re-create this satisfying slumber and boundless energy. The amount of sleep needed to maintain health and well-being varies with the individual. Some people thrive on four or five hours; others need at least eight to get through the next day. While the average falls between five to ten hours out of every twenty-four, sleep needs may change with age, physical condition and lifestyle.

In addition to the amount of sleep that is right for you, the hours during which you sleep should ideally be based on your individual body rhythms. Some people (often called "larks") naturally wake up and function best in the early daylight hours, tiring and reaching their lowest ebbs at night. Others (called "owls") find it far more satisfactory to sleep during the day, "coming alive" in the later hours and reaching the peak of productivity in the wee hours. In our 9:00 to 5:00 society, "owls" often have a difficult time adjusting to a "lark" schedule.

Whatever your body rhythms indicate, the most important factor is the *quality* of your sleep, rather than when you sleep or the number of hours you spend in bed. You'll know you've had enough *good* sleep if you wake up feeling refreshed and ready to go.

To enjoy good sleep, it's useful to understand what happens when the body rests and take steps to ensure the best sleep possible.

Sleep periods are comprised of 90- to 100-minute cycles in which four stages take place. During the first stage, body temperature and blood pressure drop, heart rate slows, muscles relax, and voluntary (conscious) thoughts slowly suspend. In this stage, the brain may initially emit fast, intense electrical impulses, sometimes producing sudden jerky movements of muscles or limbs.

In the second stage, a period of medium-deep sleep occurs. The third stage is the deepest sleep.

In the final stage, one of light sleep, great amounts of electrical energy are discharged by the brain. It is at this stage that dreams, signaled by *r*apid *e*ye *m*ovements (sometimes designated as REM), occur. Shiftings of body position are also usually more frequent at this stage.

Sleep cycles need to occur in their proper sequence throughout the sleeping period if your mind and body are to enjoy truly refreshing, restorative sleep. When you fight sleep—or when the cycles are disrupted by overtiredness, stress, physical or emotional problems, or drugs or alcohol that rob you of REM periods—you may feel that you "haven't slept a wink."

For most of us, sustained insomnia isn't a serious problem. But there are times when illness, worries, or emotional upsets throw us and our sleeping patterns out of kilter. The following suggestions for helping yourself to peaceful slumber are recommended by many sleep experts:

- Discuss sleep problems with your doctor and get a checkup to determine if there is any physical basis. However, don't jump for prescription or over-the-counter sleeping pills. They disrupt the natural stages of sleep and offer only a temporary cure for insomnia. They also may lead to drug dependency.
- Try to stop worrying about your sleeplessness. If you allow yourself to become frightened, you'll exacerbate the problem. When you are tired enough, you'll eventually sleep.
- As much as possible, follow your natural biological clock. Learn when you sleep best—and sleep *then*.
- Establish a regular time and ritual for retiring. Condition yourself to doing the same things before you go to bed so your body knows it's time to sleep.
- Avoid heavy meals and exercise before bedtime, as well as deep-sleep naps during the day. Stay awake until your regular bedtime.
- Sleep in a darkened, quiet room or wear a mask designed to shut out light.
- Find a firm, comfortable mattress that supports your body but doesn't hamper movement.
- If you share your bed with a partner, you may need to sleep separately for a while to help you both relax. On the other hand, sex is highly regarded as a relaxant and sleep-inducing activity.
- If you wear bedclothes, be sure they're loose enough to allow freedom of movement and circulation.
- Try to maintain your bedroom temperature at the optimum level for sleep—around 60–65° F—with enough moisture in the air to prevent drying of skin and mucous membranes. Use air conditioners sparingly in summer; a humidifier is useful in dry heat.
- To prevent accumulation of fluids in your eyes and cheeks, sleep on your back and/or raise the head of your bed by placing a 2 × 4 under two of the bed's legs.
- Avoid coffee, colas, tea, and chocolate prior to bedtime. They contain caffeine, which is a stimulant. Milk, cheese, or a few calcium supplements often serve as natural tranquilizers.
- Don't abuse alcohol, or use it as a sedative. Like sleeping pills, it robs you of natural sleep and disrupts the important dream stages of sleep.

- While reading, recalling pleasant experiences, and so forth may be helpful for some, these activities often cause more harm than good if they are mentally stimulating. If you stay up all night reading or planning your vacation, you may have a rough time functioning the next day.
- Proper nutrition, regular exercise, and relaxation during the day should lead to restful sleep. If something is bothering you, try to solve the problem—or at least do what you can do and accept what you cannot change.

For serious sleep disorders, you would be well-advised to contact a clinic that specializes in the evaluation and treatment of problems in this area.

Cleaning/Moisturizing/Protecting

Keeping the skin clean and sealing in natural moisture are the final elements for maintaining a youthful appearance.

Finding the skin regimen best suited to your needs will require trial and error. When trying any new product, buy the smallest size and see how your skin responds before investing in a large quantity. There are many good products available—and not always the most expensive—to help you care for your skin. For example, if applied sparingly and massaged into the skin, pure petroleum jelly can be as good a moisturizer as more costly "magic formula" products.

Despite advertising claims extolling the virtues of various proteins, vitamins, hormones, and other exotic-sounding ingredients, there generally are only two items that count in a moisturizer: water and oil. The latter may be animal, vegetable, or mineral, all of which are equally effective. The only basic difference in moisturizers is the consistency—whether a heavier cream or lighter lotion—and this factor makes no difference in the results produced.

As stated earlier, moisturizers do not put moisture into your skin. Only you can do that by drinking plenty of water and by patting some water on your skin before applying a moisturizer, which then seals in the water.

Everyone should use a moisturizer, even men and women with oily skin (for whom oil-free products have been developed). Some kind of toning lotion also is helpful for all but dry-skin types. This may be called an astringent, clarifying lotion, or freshener. The only basic difference is in alcohol content, which is greatest in astringents (up to 60 percent) and lowest in fresheners (as low as 2 percent). Astringents are best for oily skin and the other products best for normal and combination skin.

Here are guidelines for cleaning the four basic skin types (these suggestions apply to both men and women):

- *For oily skin:*
  *Use a soap or cleanser formulated for oily skin.
  *Use a textured washcloth or abrasive sponge and firm pressure (but don't overdo it!). Removal of all dead cells, surface dirt, and oil will help fight blemishes.
  *Wash two or three times a day, depending on how oily your skin is.
  *Rinse very thoroughly. Then wipe oily areas with an astringent-dipped cotton ball. Some alcohol-based astringents may be too harsh and drying. You may want to use them on your entire face once a day and on your nose, chin, and forehead more often.
  *Once a week, use cleansing grains to unclog pores and rid the skin of dead cells that hold dirt and oil on the surface.
  *With both astringents and grains, avoid eye areas. This skin is very delicate, so any pulling may lead to wrinkles. Top off your cleansing routine with a light, non-oily moisturizer. Avoid heavy makeup. Use a water-based foundation or bronzer and refresh during the day to keep oily shine to a minimum.
  *Men: Avoid cleansing grains directly after shaving (they may be too irritating). A splash of non-oily aftershave will soothe the skin and keep down oily shine.

- *For dry skin:*
  *Be gentle but thorough. Use a superfatted soap or dry skin cleanser; avoid detergents and deodorant soaps. Gently use a cloth to rid skin of all dead cells and keep your pores very clean.
  *Use warm, *never hot*, water and rinse every bit of soap from your face. Pat dry.
  *While the skin is still slightly damp, apply a rich moisturizer to seal in as much water as possible.
  *Apply extra moisturizer to the eye areas, cheeks, mouth, and neck. You might carry a small bottle with you and keep some in the office, too. If you spend a lot of time in air conditioning or dry heat, you may need additional applications during the day.
  *Stay away from astringents, especially alcohol-based ones, as they are too harsh for dry skin. A mild toner or freshener once a day, or every other day, should do the trick.
  *Use cream or oil-base makeup and foundation or bronzer, but lightly to avoid clogging pores.
  *Men: Be particularly careful when shaving. Use a shaving cream

that will lubricate your skin well (or pre-shave lotion if you prefer an electric shaver).

For normal skin:

*Use a milky, non-alkaline soap and textured washcloth once or twice a day. Clean thoroughly—you, too, need to remove all surface dirt and dead skin cells.

*Rinse, pat dry, and lightly apply moisturizer.

*Twice a week, you may want to use cleansing grains or astringents for extra cleansing strength.

*You can use just about any makeup and foundation or bronzer that lasts best and cleans off easily.

• *For combination skin:*

*Follow the oily-skin guidelines for the oily areas, and the dry-skin care tips for dry areas. Women need to be careful in choosing the right makeup for this skin type. You may need powder for the "T-zone" (forehead, nose, and chin), cream blush and shadow for the cheeks and eyes, and so on. Try different types—or ask the advice of a qualified skin care specialist.

Whatever your skin type, if you're using soap on your face, you'll want to select a mild one. A study conducted by Dr. Albert M. Kligman, Professor of Dermatology at the University of Pennsylvania School of Medicine,[29] rated some of the most popular soaps. Graded from 0 to 10 (with 1 or under as the mildest and 5 or more the harshest), the soaps were rated as follows:

Dove	0.5	Jergens	3.3
Purpose	2.3	Cuticura	3.9
Dial	2.4	Basis	4.0
Alpha Keri	2.5	Irish Spring	4.0
Fels Naptha	2.6	Zest	6.1
Neutrogena	2.8	Camay	6.4
Ivory	2.8	Lava	6.4
Lowila	3.2		

Don't overlook the skin directly below your face—the neck. Because the skin in this area is usually thin and sensitive, the signs of aging may appear here before any other parts of the body. While wrinkles and sagging skin may be caused by poor posture or sleep habits that cause hunching and scrunching of the neck, they're most often the result of neglect.

Clean your neck just as gently and thoroughly as your face. Use your moisturizer and/or night cream, massaged into the neck with upward strokes. Avoid harsh astringents or colognes because of their high alcohol content, which can dry the skin.

Facials and masks are part of a basic skin care and protection regime. While these don't prevent wrinkles, they can make your skin feel fresh, smooth, and clean. Women, and more and more men, are treating themselves to professional facials. The procedure is used to remove dirt and oils from the pores and to generally deep-clean and moisturize the skin.

A professional facial (and many home varieties) usually consists of massage, steaming with herbs, deep cleansing, and any other treatments geared to your skin type and specific problems. Many salons employ trained estheticians who can safely remove blackheads and pimples—but serious acne should always be treated by a dermatologist.

Many men and women experience a psychological boost after a facial. They find these treatments relaxing, and their skin takes on a healthy-looking glow. Often salons include makeup sessions and instructions for skin care techniques that can be used at home by both male and female clients.

Kay Acuazzo says that the number of men consulting her about skin care treatment has doubled in the past few years, an observation echoed by numerous other estheticians around the country. Often, male clients first come for a facial or other treatment as the result of prodding by their wives or women friends, says Ms. Acuazzo. When they learn how much better their skin looks and feels, they continue enthusiastically. Such well-known personalities as Dustin Hoffman, Gabe Kaplan, Gene Simmons of KISS, Paul Newman, O. J. Simpson, and former astronaut Scott Carpenter have taken advantage of and benefited from professional skin care sessions.

Ms. Acuazzo believes that one of the reasons increasing numbers of businessmen are seeking skin care advice is stepped-up job competition with women. "Women executives know they have to look good to land a job or get ahead in their career. They are accustomed to taking extra-special care of their skin and grooming. I believe this is having an impact on men. We find that men are wearing more makeup—not rouge or eyeshadow but base makeup, such as bronzers, for a healthier, more vigorous appearance."

If you'd like to give yourself a facial at home, begin with a steaming to deep-clean and unclog facial pores.

(1) Half fill a shallow, wide-mouth, four-quart pan with water.

(2) Bring the water to a boil, and remove from the heat.

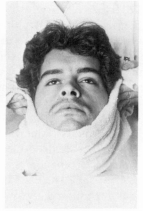
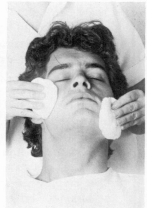

Before   Steamed Towel   Cleanse

(3) Apply eye cream and, if you have dry skin, add moisturizer to your entire face.

(4) Cover your head and the pan with a towel to hold in the steam.

For oily skin, follow this procedure twice a week, holding your face about twenty inches from the pan for eight to ten minutes. For dry skin, once a week is sufficient, but hold your head about two feet from the pan for only three to five minutes. For normal or combination skin, steam once a week for eight to ten minutes with your head about two feet from the pan.

Afterward, try one of the many pre-mixed products geared for different skin types. The four basic kinds of masks are:

- *Clay*. The base is mineral clay that hardens on the skin and absorbs oil and dirt. This type can be good for oily skin but should probably be professionally applied since it may cause broken capillaries and reportedly results in headaches in some cases.

- *Moisturizing*. These are usually formed from jelly-like moisturizers, often mixed with protein, and are used to moisturize as well as cleanse. Dry and normal skin types can benefit from a moisturizing mask.

Shave

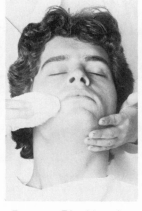

Remove Blackheads

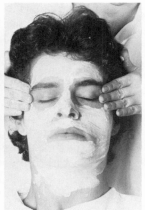

Mask

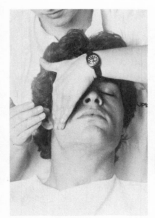

Massage

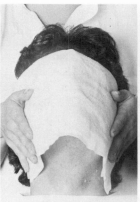

Steamed Towel

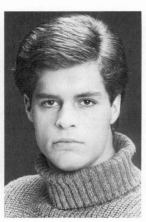

After

- *Peel-off.* Generally made from a rubber or wax base, these masks are applied as a cream or lotion, then allowed to dry and peeled off in one piece. Experts recommend peel-off masks for slightly oily or normal skin.

- *Massaging.* Formed from some kind of plastic and applied as a cream or lotion, massaging masks are removed when dry by rubbing. They are especially good for removing dirt and superficial dead skin cells from oily and normal skin. Be careful not to rub too hard.

You also can whip up your own exotic, luxurious facial treatment products with the aid of a blender and a supply of fresh fruits, vegetables, and oils. The advantages: you know exactly what's in them; they'll always be fresh, since they're made from perishable foods and need to be mixed for each use; and taking the time to prepare and enjoy them will help you relax.

The following are samples of simple, refreshing skin care products you might like to try. Men and women can use them, but as with any new product, you should do a patch test before applying the mixture to your whole face. Foods contain minerals, acids, and chemicals that may irritate your skin as much as any product you purchase in a store.

- *For Oily Skin*
  Avocado Cleanser
  Peel and mash half a soft avocado and mix it with ¼ cup of cornmeal. After washing your face, apply the mixture, either to trouble spots or to your entire face. Rub gently for a few minutes, then rinse well with a washcloth. Splash with witch hazel or skin freshener.

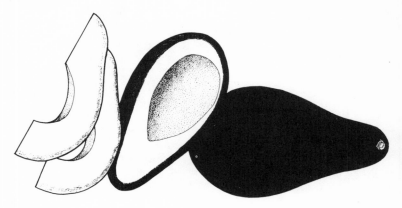

Oatmeal or Cornmeal Paste Mask
Mix raw oatmeal or cornmeal with a little warm water and apply it to your face after washing. Leave on for 15 minutes; rinse well with warm water, then cool water.

Lemon or Cider Vinegar Rinse

Dilute lemon juice or cider vinegar in water and rinse your face after washing. These rinses will help remove soap and excess oil from your face. Rinse with clear water afterwards.

To Lemon or Not to Lemon

As with all makeup and cleansing preparations, a small number of people are allergic to lemons. If you're not sure about you and lemons, try this test: Squeeze a couple of drops of lemon on a cotton ball, apply to a small patch of skin, then wait 24 hours. If any irritation occurs, better not try these treatments.

- ## For Dry Skin

Apricot Facial

Soak 6 sun-dried apricots in boiled water; let stand overnight, covered. The next morning, puree apricots in a blender with 5 seedless green grapes. If desired, sprinkle powdered milk in the mixture to thicken it. Spread on face with fingers and let set until dry (about 12–15 minutes). Rinse well with warm water.

Avocado–Egg Yolk Mask

Beat an egg yolk well, then add ½ an avocado which has been peeled and mashed. Blend in a blender until smooth. Cleanse face and neck, then apply mask to entire area. Let dry for 15–20 minutes. Rinse thoroughly with warm water.

Creamy Peach Facial

Place ½ peach, washed, cubed, and peeled in a blender with 1 egg white and 2 tablespoons cream. Blend until liquified. Smooth on face and allow to dry. Rinse with warm, then cool water.

Honeydew Mask

Mash ½ of a honeydew melon and apply to your face as a mask. Rinse with warm water; be sure all of the melon is removed.

Honey

Spread pure, unfiltered honey on your skin. Wait until it becomes tacky to the touch, then rinse very thoroughly.

- *For Normal Skin*
  Avocado-Cucumber
  Mask

Mash ½ a peeled avocado until it becomes a soft cream. Peel ½ a cucumber and slice it paper thin. Press out the juice (retain for a refreshing skin lotion), and add the pulp to the softened avocado. Apply to your already cleansed face and neck; let set for 15 minutes. Remove with a thorough tepid water rinse, then apply cucumber juice as a freshener.

Egg White Facial

Beat an egg white until foamy. After cleansing your face, apply the egg white and let dry (5–15 minutes). You'll need to rinse *very* well, but your face will feel wonderful.

A note on collagen: Recently a number of skin products containing the natural protein collagen have appeared on the market. The Food and Drug Administration, as well as many dermatologists, have found no evidence of benefits to consumers from the inclusion of collagen among other ingredients in various facial creams. Researchers point out that oils in these skin care products, plus exposure to oxygen, would destroy the collagen's helpful properties. Furthermore, the very small amount of collagen included in the overall formula provides a miniscule supply of this ingredient in each application.

There is a pure extract of collagen which is still under investigation. This is similar to the unadulterated collagen used for injections to plump up the skin (a use that has been approved by the FDA). According to Peter Hantz, whose company distributes Collagen-PH in the United States, "Pharmaceutical laboratories extract collagen from animal tissue and package it in individual ampules—free from any fatty substances which block skin pores and prevent the skin from breathing. The collagen doesn't come into contact with oxygen until the ampule is broken open and the collagen applied to the face and neck." Mr. Hantz believes that the active molecules in this pure form of collagen can penetrate the skin, "helping to moisturize, restore firmness, and prevent premature wrinkling."

WHETHER THE WEATHER

In considering protection of your skin, the "elements" are a primary factor. First, I strongly recommend that everyone, but especially fair-skinned, light-eyed men and women, avoid exposure to the sun and wind as much as possible. If you live in a strong-sun zone, if you work outdoors in the sun or cold, or if the sports and leisure activities you enjoy keep you in the sun for long periods—winter or summer—you should invest in a high-performance sunscreen. (People with very fair skins should use a sunblock.) Otherwise, you may pay dearly later in life for the golden tan you have now.

All skin types tend to be drier in the winter, so you may need to adjust your skin care regimen accordingly. Milder soaps, fewer baths (or quicker showers), extra moisturizers, humidifiers—all these should help you to keep your skin moist. Remember that wind can burn and chap, too, so protect yourself before going out with extra moisturizer on the lips, face, and area surrounding the eyes.

Summer brings more humidity, frequently increasing oily-skin problems. Clean as often as necessary, using your astringent or a lighter freshener during the day to reduce excess oil buildup. Dry-skin types benefit from humid air; air conditioning or dry desert sun and wind increase dryness.

I certainly don't want to discourage anyone from enjoying the wonderful benefits of the great outdoors—far from it. But too often we forget, or simply don't take the time, to care for our skin in every season. You need to realize the limitations of your skin. Pale blondes must be more careful of bright sunlight than those with darker complexions—although the idea that Blacks can't get sunburned is a myth.

The best protection from the harmful effects of ultraviolet rays—other than staying indoors—is a sunscreen or sun-block preparation. Sunscreens contain an active ingredient, most often PABA (para-aminobenzioc acid or a derivative), that absorbs the burning rays emitted by the sun. Sun-blocks, such as the zinc oxide dotting the noses of many lifeguards, are products which are so opaque that no light penetrates them. Sun-blocks offer the widest range of protection from all types of ultraviolet rays.

Sunscreens are rated according to an SPF (sun protection factor). The SPF is a quick way to determine the degree of protection provided by a product. The numbers range from 2 to 15. Fair skins that never tan should use a sunscreen with an SPF of 10–15; skins that burn, then tan, should use one in the 6–12 range; persons with dark skin and eyes who tan easily but burn occasionally would use an SPF of 2–6. The SPF numbers indicate the amount of time you can spend in the sun with a sunscreen before burning, as opposed to the amount of time you would spend unprotected before burning. For example, with a sun protection factor of 10–15, you could spend an extra 10 to 15 minutes in the sunlight, and so on. Remember that no skin, including Black skin, is immune to sunburn or to the risk of skin cancer or premature aging from overexposure and neglect.

Use sunscreens and blocks whenever you'll be exposed to strong sunlight for any length of time (even when taking a walk)—whether in a city, at the beach, or on a snow-capped mountain. Also keep in mind that the effect of exposure to sunlight is cumulative, the long-range effects being wrinkling, dryness, possible discoloration, destruction of blood vessels, the breakdown of the skin's elastic fibers, and possible skin cancer.

If you're taking medication of any kind, check with your doctor before sunning, since many medications heighten skin photosensitivity and increase the danger of burning. For the same reason, it's wise to forego perfumes, colognes, and other fragrances when sunbathing.

To minimize burns at first, use a gradual exposure schedule: 10 minutes the first day, 15 minutes the second day, and so on. Try not to begin your tan between 11:00 A.M. and 3:00 P.M., when the sun's rays are strongest.

In addition to natural sunlight, many tanning enthusiasts use ultraviolet sunlamps or the new "tanning center" to maintain a tan in winter or begin a tan for summer. The same precautions are necessary when exposing your skin to these artificially manufactured ultraviolet rays as with sunlight. Use goggles at all times, and cover all exposed skin areas with protective lotions. However, since there are no data yet concerning the possible side effects of artificial tanning, I suggest that you avoid this tanning method.

If you swim in a pool or the ocean, reapply sunscreen when you leave the water. If you burn easily, cover yourself and sit in the shade, away from the water. Water (and snow) act as reflectors. You may be in the shade, but the reflection of ultraviolet rays is just as dangerous as direct exposure.

Winter sun—at the tops of mountains, especially—will burn just as badly as summer sun. Use a moisturizing sunscreen or block on exposed areas.

PUT ON A HAPPY FACE

Before proceeding to skin disorders, let's examine the final stage
of the skin protection regimen, makeup—a subject increasingly of
interest to men as well as women.

In my years of practice, I've often been impressed with the ways
in which the skillful use of makeup enhances appearance and self-
expression. Since the face generally provides others with their first
visual impression of you, makeup can heighten the visual impact by
drawing attention to your most expressive features, usually the eyes
and mouth. The trick is to design a makeup style that is natural and
becoming to your face and personality, emphasizing the attractiveness and uniqueness of your features while minimizing imperfections.

The most important rule to observe when establishing your beauty or grooming routine is quite simple: what's good for health is good for appearance, since the way you feel and the way you look are closely interrelated. Makeup works best on healthy, well-cared for skin, and skin care experts caution that it's vital to begin good skin care and beauty habits as early in life as possible.

Fashion in makeup changes, but your goal is individuality: to balance your makeup with the clothes, hairstyle, and lifestyle you enjoy, to feel at ease and self-confident about the way you look. It may take time, experimentation, and perseverance, but once you master the subtle art of makeup, you can adapt current trends to express yourself. Looking terrific will be well worth the effort.

Several major skin care lines include bronzers, cover sticks, and powders along with the moisturizers, facial cleansers, and astringents designed for men. The secret for men, as with women, is learning to achieve a natural-looking skin tone. If you have trouble finding makeup to match your skin tones, try mixing with a lighter or darker shade, or use small amounts for contouring only.

U.S. Department of Commerce research indicates that half the men in this country now use some skin care or other grooming products.[30] So if wearing makeup makes you feel better about your appearance, by all means use it—you have plenty of company. Just remember that for men as well as women, less is more.

Beginning in your teens (a practical gift for daughters), a professional makeup and skin-care consultation is a good investment every five to ten years. Since your skin and face change as you age, your makeup and skin care program should be adjusted to meet these changes. These professionals will put you at ease. Feel free to ask questions about your bone structure, features, skin tone, and texture; take notes on how to achieve the look you want; and obtain tips on home application of makeup. This type of consultation needn't be expensive. In fact, knowing the best types and shades of makeup for you can save you from costly experimentation. Check the Yellow Pages of the phone directory or ask your hairstylist for the names of makeup specialists in your area.

Armed with this information, you'll be ready to proceed with these guidelines:

• *Step 1.* Always begin with a clean face. Apply a thin coat of *moisturizer*. At this point, you can use a *corrective underbase* to adjust skin tones (for example, your skin may have too yellow, red, or olive a cast). Using a corrective underbase neutralizes the undertones to provide a smooth, neutral finish to foundation.

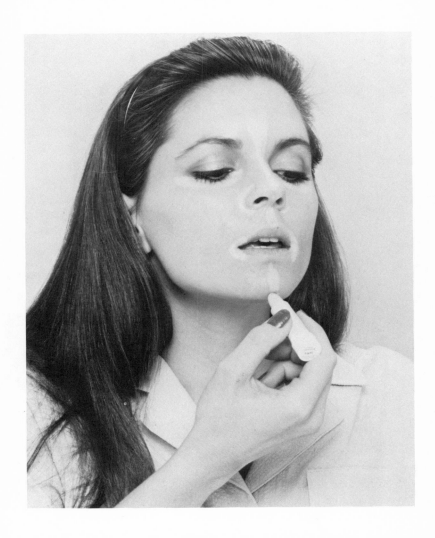

Choose an underbase as follows: correct a dark yellow (sallow) complexion with warm pink; light yellow with blue or lavender tint; olive with pink or peach; red with light green tint.

- *Step 2.* Look for areas you'd like to camouflage; for example, dark circles under the eyes, expression lines around the mouth, blemishes, red spots. The following chapters give tips on using cover-ups to correct these problems.
- *Step 3.* Once the skin is primed with moisturizer, and with underbase and cover-up if necessary, you're ready to apply *foundation.*

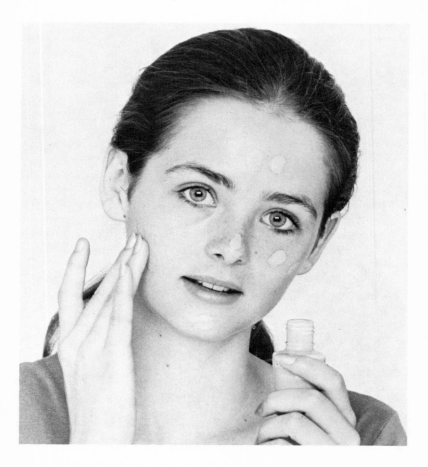

Choose a base that matches your skin. Before buying, test it on your face and neck, not on your hand; the tones are very different. For oily skin you may want to stick with a water-based foundation; dry skins get smoother coverage with an oil or cream base. Some tips on application:

    *Dot the base over one small area at a time, then blend with a slightly damp makeup sponge to prevent streaking. Use light, circular downward strokes. This will prevent buildup on facial hair and promote even coverage.

    *Blend to the hairline and feather over the jawline. If foundation color has been properly matched to face color, there should be no telltale line of demarcation between jaw and neck.

A note on Black skin: The wide range of Black skin tones poses special problems in selecting the right foundation. Products formulated for Caucasians tend to become ashy when applied to Black skin. Fortunately, cosmetic manufacturers now provide products specifically designed for Black skin tones. Even so, you may not be able to find a foundation that's a perfect match for your skin. In this case, makeup artists recommend blending several shades to create a foundation as close as possible to your own natural coloring. The trick, according to professionals, is to match the darkest *undertone* (red, orange, yellow) as well as your basic skin color.

- *Step 4.* Proceed to make up your individual features and add contours and highlights as described in the following chapters.
- *Step 5.* Add powder for the finishing touch, which gives the rest of your makeup staying power. Many professional makeup artists today prefer an airy, translucent loose powder to tinted cake varieties. This allows the tones of your foundation and contouring/ highlighting to "shine" through without any discoloration. To set your makeup, dip a soft brush into loose powder; shake a few times to remove the excess; and dust lightly over forehead, nose, and chin.

As a final touch, a mist of water will help makeup last longer. Use a fine plant sprayer or atomizer and don't try to soak your skin. Dab with a cotton ball afterwards. This is also a good pick-me-up when you're traveling by airplane, which tends to dehydrate the skin. A few spritzes of water are both refreshing and restorative.

A note on fluorescent lighting: Most offices and other businesses are illuminated by fluorescent lights, which can make the best complexion look a bit green and faded. If you spend most of your working hours exposed to fluorescent lighting, test your makeup under these conditions and adjust the colors you're using to present the most flattering appearance. Since fluorescents tend to accentuate harsh edges, careful blending and feathering out of all makeup are particularly important. Home makeup mirrors are available with different settings for fluorescent, evening (subdued), and outdoor (natural) lighting, so you can adjust your makeup for your needs of the day.

MAKEUP SAFETY TIPS

When used with caution and common sense, most cosmetic products are not particularly harmful to the average person. However, these *are* chemical preparations and should be treated with respect. Cosmetics cause an estimated 60,000 injuries each year to people's eyes, skin, and hair. As with any other chemical compound, read the package contents carefully and ask your pharmacist, cosmetologist, esthetician, or doctor about any ingredients that you think may be harmful. Follow usage directions to the letter, especially when using hair products. Here are a few additional safety tips to help minimize risks:

• Always wash your hands before applying cosmetics and keep your makeup area scrupulously clean.

• Don't keep makeup, especially eye makeup, for more than three or four months. The preservatives in these products break down very quickly.

• Don't borrow makeup. Avoid makeup counter samples that are accessible to the public unless the samples are applied from disposable palates or applicators.

• While hypoallergenic products may be useful to sensitive skins, they can still cause allergic reactions. These products are usually free of fragrances, a chief source of allergic reactions, but those who might have adverse reactions to other makeup ingredients are still susceptible. Always check with your dermatologist if you tend toward makeup allergies or are unsure about a product's contents and effects.

• Take care of your beauty and grooming tools. This will minimize the chances for harmful bacteria and soils to invade your makeup and skin—and will also add to the effectiveness and life span of the tools. Makeup brushes, particularly those used for eye makeup, should be cleaned frequently and replaced several times a year. Tap off excess powder, then swish brushes in sudsy warm water (you may need a few changes of water before all colors are removed). Rinse in clear water and pat with a towel, then allow the brushes to air dry. Soak makeup sponges in a solution of baking soda and warm water, then wash in warm sudsy water and rinse in clear water. Again, makeup sponges should be cleaned often and replaced when they begin to wear or crumble.

Makeup Chart

FACE
Foundation
_____

Powder
_____

TEMPLES/NOSE/JAW
Contour
_____

Highlight
_____

CHEEKS
Contour
_____

Highlight
_____

MOUTH
Lip Liner
_____

Lip Colors
_____

_____

_____

EYES
Eyebrow Pencil
_____

Highlight Colors
_____

_____

_____

Contour Colors
_____

_____

Lid Color Colors
_____

_____

_____

Eyeliner
_____

Mascara
_____

Undereye Concealer
_____

4
LENDING A HAND TO NATURE

"It is the common wonder of all men, how among so many millions of faces, there should be none alike."[31]

Sometimes, despite the best of care, our skin needs a little extra help. Fortunately, skin treatment procedures and materials are constantly improving. Thanks to modern chemistry and technology, skin care and treatment professionals have an impressive arsenal with which to combat the wide range of skin disorders.

These disorders may appear in a variety of forms, some more serious than others. Among the most prevalent skin problems, along with the newest means of dealing with them, are the following.

ACNE

According to esthetician Ann Keane, persistent problems with blackheads or whiteheads (which, along with pimples, are the main forms of acne) are among the primary reasons men and women consult a skin care specialist. Ms. Keane estimates that these major skin disorders affect virtually everyone at some point in their lives. "Even I have them occasionally," she says, "and I have dry skin and take meticulous care of it with daily cleansing and moisturizing and regular facials."

Because these skin eruptions come from within, there's no way to get rid of them once they appear. In appearance, whiteheads have no visible opening, while blackheads do. In blackheads, normal skin pigment forms a dark color. Both are clogs of oil, skin cells, and bacteria in the pore. For the milder forms the sediment can be removed, but this should only be done by a trained skin-care specialist in order to avoid the risk of infection. Usually this is done by a dermatologist or a well-trained esthetician. More severe acne should always be treated by a dermatologist.

Although acne is generally associated with younger persons (health surveys suggest that at least 85 percent of Americans between the ages of 12 and 25 are affected by this skin disease), acne is increasing among older adults—even those in their 40s.

Dr. Alan R. Shalita, chairman of New York's Downstate Medical Center Dermatology Department, says that in its most severe form, acne can "cause considerable physical and emotional distress. Acne lesions usually begin to appear at a time in life when young people are making the transition from childhood to adult life and attempting to establish an identity for themselves. The burden of a sometimes physically disfiguring skin disease often places significant emotional stress on the individual."

Acne sufferers shouldn't heed the old adage to "wait until you're 21 and it all goes away." Persistent acne should be treated early in order to try to avoid scarring. Many adults today still bear the scars of teenage acne on their faces because they didn't seek early treatment.

A major factor in the occurrence of acne in adolescent boys and girls is the rising levels of testosterone (the male hormone), which causes an increase in the size and activity of the sebaceous (oil) glands. Stress and environmental pollution may be other contributors to acne, although there is no conclusive evidence on these points so far.

Contrary to popular belief, acne isn't an infection, although bacteria in the canals leading from the sebaceous glands to the skin's surface may cause irritation. Acne also isn't caused by specific foods—another common myth. However, some people do have what Dr. Shalita refers to as "idiosyncrasies to certain foods." If you always seem to break out after eating shellfish, chocolate, fried dishes or any other food, you should avoid these items.

Acne is not caused by dirt, but proper cleansing is the first step in home treatment. You should first wash with a non-abrasive cleanser, and then apply a lotion, cream, or gel containing sulfur, salicylic acid, or benzoyl peroxide. Overwashing is to be avoided. Dr. Shalita warns: "A maximum of three cleanings per day is all that's needed if the skin is oily. Sometimes those with extremely oily skin find an astringent cleanser useful."

Sometimes a dermatologist will prescribe low doses of antibiotics or other drugs. For the more severe inflammatory forms of acne, Dr. Shalita says tetracycline is still "the antibiotic of choice because of its wide margin of safety, established efficacy, and low cost." Alternatives include erythromycin, clindamycin, and minocycline. To help reduce the chances of possible side-effects, including diarrhea, constipation, fatigue, and vaginal yeast infections, patients should adhere strictly to their doctor's instructions for taking any type of antibiotic pill.

The same antibiotics now have been approved by the FDA for direct application to the skin. Although they don't produce results as quickly as when taken in pill form, they won't cause the side-effects mentioned above. Among the more recent advances in acne treatment is a topical vitamin A acid. For use in treating many forms of acne problems, this retoniac acid is applied directly to the skin and incites the discharge of the contents of the pustule with no resultant scarring.

POCKMARKS

A pitted scarring often results from chicken pox or neglect of severe acne. This situation can be substantially improved by three different techniques: dermabrasion, liquid silicone or collagen injections, and skin grafts.

1. *Dermabrasion* is a method of mechanically removing superficial layers of skin to produce a smoother, more regular surface. No incisions are made, since the procedure consists of "sanding" the skin with a high-speed drill and planing discs. This technique can be used to minimize the difference between the pitted areas and the normal skin surface. I combine dermabrasion and boring with a face lift procedure to further reduce the depth of facial depressions. To achieve this, I clean out pockmarks by boring (in much the same way a dentist drills to remove cavities), then stitch together the sides of the pockmarks with dissolvable sutures.
2. *Injections* of surgical liquid silicone or the newer liquid collagen can help reduce the evidence of deep, saucer-shaped acne scarring by plumping up the skin. Because it's a synthetic material, silicone isn't absorbed into the body and sometimes will shift posi-

tion. Collagen, as explained earlier, is a natural protein. Upon injection, it begins to colonize with existing cells and blood vessels until it becomes a part of the body's normal dermal layer. Collagen injections are useful in reducing vertical frown and laugh lines and the tiny vertical age lines on the upper lip. They aren't effective for "ice-pick" (deep, narrow holes) acne scarring or horizontal lines, nor as a replacement for a standard face lift. I include a series of collagen injections as standard part of the post-operative treatment for my cosmetic surgery patients, since this enhances the surgical improvements.

Both silicone and collagen injections have Food and Drug Administration approval and both techniques are restricted to physicians who have been specially trained in their use.

3. *Skin grafts* can improve "ice-pick" scarring. With the use of a special instrument, skin removed from behind the earlobe is used to fill in the pockmarks that have been surgically cut out.

PIGMENTATION PROBLEMS

Skin discoloration can occur for a variety of reasons, says Dr. Paul Lazar, President of the Dermatology Foundation and a professor of clinical dermatology at Chicago's Northwestern University Medical School. Blacks are particularly susceptible to dark spots caused by acne or some other kinds of inflammation or burns. Although darkening occurs on Caucasian or Oriental skins for the same reasons, it may be less noticeable than on Blacks. For all three groups, however, the color differences may be more disturbing to some individuals than to others. Sometimes the discolorations can be minimized by using a pigment-inhibiting bleach.

Another pigmentation problem that can significantly affect Blacks is vitiligo. In this case, pigment cells have ceased to produce pigment, resulting in light patches on the skin. Again, this disease is encountered by Caucasians and Orientals but may not cause such a marked difference in their appearance. In some cases, vitiligo is treated with drugs and ultraviolet light to stimulate pigment cell production.

An effective cosmetic remedy for vitiligo, liver spots, a variety of birthmarks (including port wine stains), freckles, burns, and other blemishes and scars is Covermark. Although I don't normally discuss brand name products, the remarkable camouflaging properties of Covermark are so widely recommended by surgeons and dermatologists that I believe it should be mentioned by name. It was developed more than 40 years ago by Lydia O'Leary, herself the victim of a large, disfiguring birthmark. When she sought a sales position with the retailer for whom she worked, her employer rejected Ms. O'Leary's request because he didn't want her exposed to the customers. In order to achieve her goal in retailing, Ms. O'Leary and a friend began experimenting with formulas for a cream to conceal the birthmark. The result, Covermark, became the first cosmetic item ever granted a United States patent.

Since its invention, Covermark has enabled countless men and women to put their best face forward, quite literally changing their lives in many cases. The line now includes twelve shades of water-

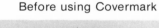

Before using Covermark

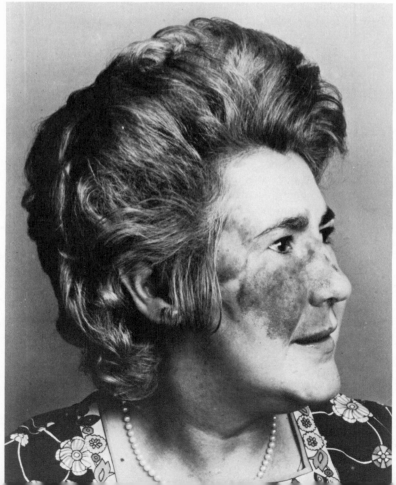

proof foundation, a cover stick for concealing temporary blemishes, blushers, shading cream, a setting powder, and a gray toner for male beard areas. Generally available through department stores, these products are water- and sun-proof. Proper application is important to the results created with these products, so you should ask for a demonstration of how to apply them to your face.

A relatively new surgical procedure for substantially removing certain kinds of skin blemishes and lightening the color of port-wine birthmarks involves the use of laser beams—powerful light rays that can be finely focused to generate heat. When the laser beams are directed into discolored skin areas, they destroy blood vessels near the skin's surface. This reduces blood flow and results in lighter

After using Covermark

skin. While this technique will not erase birthmarks and is not recommended for those under the age of 17, it does offer the hope of a better appearance for many adults who suffer from unsightly port-wine stains. This procedure may not be as successful for non-Caucasians, whose birthmarks are turned gray by the laser beam; however, a preference for this or the darker shade is a matter of individual taste.

Traditionally, attempts to treat this kind of birthmark with plastic surgery haven't always been successful, since they sometimes result in a raised area that patients find more unattractive than the original problem.

DANDRUFF

Seborrheic dermatitis (the medical term for dandruff) isn't confined to the scalp, says Dr. Lazar. It also occurs on the face. "This often is misinterpreted, especially by women, as being dry skin because one of the symptoms is flaking. The cause of the problem is an inflammation, which may produce redness in addition to scaling around the nose, mouth and eyebrow areas. For women, this poses special problems since they have to use oily makeup to achieve a smooth-looking surface over the flaking area—and the oily base frequently compounds the problem."

HYPERTROPHIC SCARS (Keloids)

Most commonly found among Blacks and dark-skinned Caucasians, the condition commonly known as keloids results from an abnormal growth of scar tissue around burn, surgical, acne, and other scars. Most often this condition can be improved by the injection of a steroid that flattens out the keloid.

PSORIASIS

An estimated 1 of every 50 Americans is a victim of this chronic disease, which results in thick, silvery-scaled patches of reddened skin on any part of the body or head. To date, medical science hasn't discovered either the cause or the cure for psoriasis; however, the condition can be treated to reduce or control its effects. If you think you may have this disease, do consult a doctor. There's no reason to suffer needlessly.

MOLES AND OTHER GROWTHS

Sometimes facial moles are considered "beauty marks" (Gloria Swanson emphasizes one next to her mouth), but most people who have these growths regard them as blemishes. Removal of moles is a relatively simple procedure, with the precise method determined by the type and location of the mole involved. For moles or any other kind of facial growth, early diagnosis of the origin is advisable, so see a dermatologist for an analysis.

SIGNS OF AGING

Lines and wrinkles that begin creeping up on us as we get older result from heredity, loss of skin tone, and a variety of other factors, most of which have already been discussed. In addition to dermabrasion and silicone or collagen injections, two additional methods for reducing the impact of aging on your appearance are chemosurgery and face lift surgery.

Chemosurgery

A chemical peel is used to remove wrinkles and rejuvenate the skin. Because it involves the application of strong acids to the face, a deep chemical peel should only be done by a highly qualified professional. Unfortunately, there currently are no licensing laws or medical certification requirements to govern the qualifications of those who are performing these procedures. The formula is readily available, and in too many instances, totally unqualified persons— both doctors and lay practitioners—have been taking advantage of the lack of regulation to set themselves up as chemosurgery specialists. Many plastic surgeons, dermatologists, and estheticians are doing chemical peels, but you should check very carefully before making a choice in this area. If done improperly, chemosurgery can result in scarring, skin discoloration, or toxic reactions.

Before deciding to have chemosurgery, discuss both the procedure and the chemicals that are used by the specialist you're interviewing. For a thorough investigation of chemosurgery, I suggest you read *Face-lifts* by Norma Lee Browning.[32]

Face-lift Surgery

Although we can't make a middle-aged man or woman look like a 20-year-old, a face lift can restore more youthful contours to an aging face. Once confined almost exclusively to the rich and famous,

Before · After

face lifts have gained increasing acceptance with people in all areas of our society. Especially in a highly competitive job market, men and women know that a youthful and vigorous appearance can be a real benefit.

Whether for professional or personal reasons (or both), large numbers of men and women are enjoying the results of cosmetic surgery. However, until recently, having a face lift was strictly a "hush-hush" procedure: even your best friends weren't told, although they probably guessed. Today, many people are discussing their cosmetic-surgery experiences openly, comparing notes on the results, and recommending surgeons who are considered particularly skillful in creating pleasing aesthetic effects. Much credit for this new frankness goes to performers such as Phyllis Diller and the Gabor ladies, and to former First Lady Betty Ford and author Truman Capote, who quite happily talk about the changes wrought through their cosmetic surgery. Beauty expert Luciana Avedon and actress Audrey Hepburn are other proponents of cosmetic surgery.

Many of my patients express the fear of being passed over for promotion and other job-related factors, as their reasons for having a face lift. As an insurance company executive told me, "I look like a poor actuarial risk for my age. That's bad for our business." Often

Before   After

men and women who have kept their bodies in good condition through a regular exercise program and proper diet find themselves with a face that belies the rest of their appearance. An example was the prominent attorney who complained of looking like a "droopy old man," despite his ability to trounce tennis opponents twenty years younger than he.

Men and women in the political field also have a vested interest in presenting the best possible face to their constituency. For example, Eleanor McGovern had a face lift prior to her husband's presidential bid.

The uplifting effect of a face lift can turn back the clock as much as ten years, but it won't stop it. The forces of gravity continue to act on the less elastic, aging skin, which means that the result of the lift generally will last only four to eight years. As I advise my patients, the results and lifespan of a face lift depend on many individual factors, including the following.

• Skin type and tone, along with bone structure, vary dramatically. Slender individuals with prominent bone structure and thin skin display more dramatic results than persons with thick skin and softer bone structure.

• Heredity and individual body chemistry play an important role in

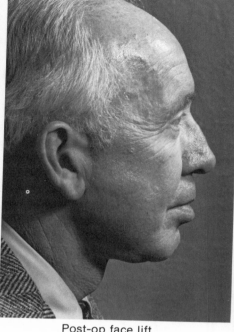

Pre-op face lift

Post-op face lift

the aging process. Members of some families seem to begin exhibiting the sags, bags and lines associated with aging at a relatively young age, while members of other families retain substantially unmarred faces well into middle age.

- Fat deposits in the facial area may be low, normal, or high—all of which will influence the results of your face lift.
- Lifestyle and environment also influence the condition of your face pre- and post-face lift. For some people, the aging process has been accelerated due to overexposure to the sun; excessive use of alcohol, tobacco products, and other chemicals; a high-stress occupation; and so forth. Such individuals are advised to modify these habits or conditions for the best results following their face lift.

A face lift will remove hanging skin and excess underlying fatty tissue that makes the skin droopy and wrinkled. At the same time, it is possible to refine the profile by reshaping the nose, augmenting the chin, and removing excess skin on the neck (the "turkey gobbler" effect).

Face lift surgery will alleviate, but not remove, the deep folds extending from the nose to the mouth and the mouth to the chin (nasolabial folds), and will not correct frown lines on the forehead. Dermabrasion is the best method of correcting nasolabial folds. Frown lines can be improved with a forehead lift. (These techniques are discussed further in Chapters 6, 7, and 8.) Also, a blepharoplasty (eye lift) often increases the aesthetic benefits of a face lift.

The face lift procedure involves making an incision along the lines shown in the illustration below. The skin is detached from the underlying tissue and pulled up, the excess skin trimmed, excess fat beneath the chin and jaw removed (if necessary) and the new, "tighter" shape of the face stitched into place.

Patients aren't able to fully appreciate the results of a face lift for about three months, during which time swelling and tightness subside. Because of this time lapse, it's fairly common for face lift patients to experience bouts of depression during the healing period. So this is one of the possible side effects for which you should be prepared.

Because they'll be dealing with a "new face," I generally send female patients for a consultation with an esthetician and makeup specialist to determine how to further enhance their face lift with makeup designed for their changed appearance. These professionals also can guide men and women patients in the best skin care program for maintaining their more youthful appearance—an im-

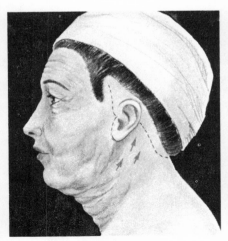

Pre-op face lift

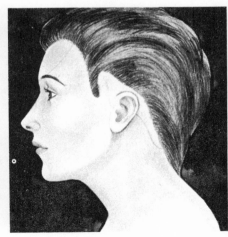

Post-op face lift

portant follow-up procedure. Women generally can begin using eye makeup five days after the sutures are removed. Full facial makeup can be resumed about a week to ten days following suture removal.

Many face-lift patients decide to complete their renovations with a new hairstyle and/or color. You can wash your hair two days after surgery and have it dyed, straightened, or permed two weeks following the operation.

Possible complications associated with face-lift surgery are hair loss at the suture sites near the scalp (usually a temporary condition and one that can be rectified) and numbness on parts of the face (generally disappears after about six months). In very rare instances, a facial nerve may be damaged, causing weakness or loss of motion in the facial muscle.

A note on retoniac acid: As discussed earlier in this chapter, vitamin A acid already is accepted as an effective treatment for acne. In addition, renowned dermatologist Albert M. Kligman is studying the use of a diluted form of the acne preparation for possible daily application to damaged or aging skin. Dr. Kligman cautions that retoniac acid won't substantially change your appearance. What it will do is improve the quality of sun-damaged skin and reduce the early stages of wrinkling by increasing the turnover of skin cells. He says: "There are demonstrable benefits for middle-aged people, including those with face lifts who don't want rough skin now that they've had it re-draped. I think about the age of 45 or 50 would be a good time to begin using vitamin A acid in the same manner that people now apply moisturizer on a daily basis." Dr. Kligman says that daily treatment of the skin with retoniac acid for two to three weeks prior to having a chemical peel produces better healing.

His research into this preparation, which he combines with a moisturizing agent, is still in its preliminary stages and hasn't been presented to the Food and Drug Administration for approval yet. However, Dr. Kligman believes we'll eventually be able to purchase retoniac acid products as easily as we now obtain other skin care preparations.

5

THE RIGHT FRAME

"Then hadst thou had an excellent head of hair."[33]

Perhaps the most beloved—and beleaguered—symbol of youth and allure is our hair. It's celebrated in song, glorified in poetry, idealized in myth. Most mortals either don't have enough, have too much that's too curly or straight—or can't do a thing with it. Graying or yellowing may be an unhappy reminder of advancing age. The long and the short of it is: beautiful hair creates the right frame for your face and definitely adds to your personal appeal.

Hair is probably the world's first miracle fiber. It can be washed, waved, tinted, straightened, brushed, combed, teased—and survive. But to do more than survive, hair needs care. Like skin, our hair responds to diet, emotional state, environment, and rest. The color and texture are inherited traits, as are degree of oiliness or dryness, curl, and hair-loss patterns.

Hair consists of proteins and minerals. It grows in cycles, and by the time you actually see it, it is essentially "dead tissue." The part that grows is underneath the skin (follicles); what you see on the surface are hair shafts. Most hairs have life cycles of two to six years, consisting of growing and resting phases that follow no particular pattern. As older hairs fall out, they are replaced by new ones—which explains the daily hair loss we all experience.

Each follicle has six oil glands that lubricate the scalp and shafts. The shafts have three layers: cuticle, cortex, and an inner core known as the medulla.

HAIR FOLLICLE IN SCALP

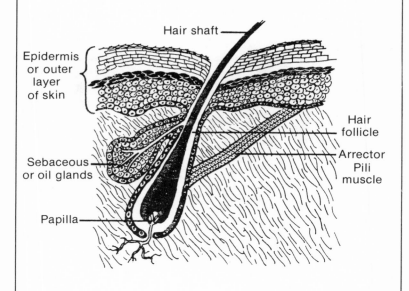

Hair shaft

Epidermis or outer layer of skin

Hair follicle

Sebaceous or oil glands

Arrector Pili muscle

Papilla

THE HAIR SHAFT

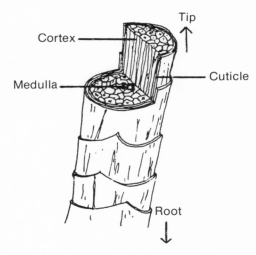

Cortex

Tip

Medulla

Cuticle

Root

Depending on the amount of oil produced, hair tends to be oily, dry, or normal. These conditions really apply to the scalp. An oily scalp has excess oil that covers the hair surfaces, giving them a greasy look and feel. Dry scalps underproduce oil. Normal oil production provides hair with just enough oil to keep it shiny-looking and manageable.

Hair texture and thickness will also affect care and styling methods. Coarse hair is made up of strands that are large in diameter; it has a lot of body, but may be wiry and dry. Fine hairs are small in diameter. They're also pliable, but may go limp and be difficult to maintain in certain styles. Either texture can be thick or thin in bulk, curly or straight. Cleansing, brushing, straightening, curling, and coloring techniques will affect the look and feel of your hair.

Hair is very much affected by seasonal or atmospheric changes. Increased humidity helps dry hair, makes curly hair frizzy, and increases problems for oily hair.

In general, washing less frequently with a milder shampoo aids dry hair exposed to dry climates, sun, and wind. Protective scarves and hats, as well as conditioners or oil treatments, will also help keep hair manageable.

Oily hair may need to be washed more often in hot or humid climates, especially after swimming, running, tennis, or other activities that increase perspiration and oil production. Very dry weather may reduce oil build-up.

Normal hair may need increased conditioning in winter, more shampooing in summer.

Damaged or bleached hair will need special attention; sun, chlorine in pools, and salt water can wreak havoc on your hair color. Try to avoid all of these, or wear bathing caps, scarves, and hats for protection.

A note on dandruff: Almost all of us get it, but nobody has invented a cure for it. Dandruff (the itching, flaking scalp condition so often identified by white flecks of skin dusted over the shoulders) generally can be controlled by frequent washing with either regular or medicated shampoo. If this doesn't alleviate the problem, you should consult a dermatologist who can determine whether you really have dandruff or some other scalp problem, such as seborrhea (an inflammation of the oil glands) or psoriasis (discussed in the preceding chapter).

KEEPING IT CLEAN

As with skin, cleansing is the foundation for your hair care program. Choose a shampoo to suit your hair type. Fortunately, there are many safe, effective products you can use to control dandruff and clean oily, dry, normal, and tinted or damaged hair.

The basic ingredients in shampoos are water, some type of sulphate (the fewer listed, the gentler the product), and a detergent to strip away dirt and grease. In addition, shampoos generally contain foaming agents to produce lather which contributes nothing to their cleaning ability. Other common additives are conditioners, such as silicone or lanoline; fragrances; coloring agents; and some type of oil. Ingredients such as proteins, placenta, herbs, beer, eggs, and avocado may sound enticing but, in reality, contribute nothing to the effectiveness of a shampoo because they're so quickly rinsed away.

For oily hair, select a ph- (acid-) balanced shampoo with fewer oils. For dry hair, choose a gentle, alcohol-free shampoo with higher oil content. Read the labels, and buy small or trial sizes until you find the right shampoo for your hair, so you won't be stuck with a huge container. If a shampoo leaves your hair brittle, dull, and listless, it's not for you.

Shampoo as often as necessary (see chart for guidelines). Hair care specialists from Clairol recommend two sudsings and two rinses for everyone. They also suggest massaging your scalp while shampooing—both for the pleasant feeling it produces and for the benefits to your hair. Rinsing is the secret to clean hair. Leftover shampoo will cause a dull film on the hair that attracts dirt and oil. Rinse several times, using warm water for the first two rinses and cool water for the final one. Many dull-haired complainers are themselves at fault for skipping the vital second and third rinsings.

GUIDELINES FOR HAIR CARE

HAIR TYPE	CHARACTERISTICS	HAIR CARE PROGRAM
NORMAL	Is neither too dry nor too oily. Can go several days without shampooing and still look good.	Shampoo frequently. Use an after-shampoo creme rinse or conditioner, and deep-condition at least once a month.
OILY	Can feel matted down the day after shampooing, looking stringy and limp.	Shampoo every day; deep-condition once a month.
DRY	Tends to be flyaway, be prone to electricity when brushed, and be prone to split ends and breakage.	Shampoo every 2–3 days, or as often as needed. Use creme rinse or conditioner after shampooing. Deep-condition twice a month or more.

When towel drying, blot the hair gently. Never rub, pull, or twist the hair. Comb out tangles with a wide-tooth comb, not a brush. Be gentle: hair is most vulnerable to breakage when wet.

To keep hair fresh between the wet washes, an instant shampoo is excellent. It's a cleansing spray mist that keeps hair clean without destroying the set. Spray it through the hair, fluff, then brush. Instant shampoos blot up excess oil, a special boon for oily hair.

A note on cornrows: Men and women with cornrows are advised to rinse their hair each day (securing the cornrows with a stocking cap) and shampoo at least once a week. Shampoo should be lathered on your hands, then very gently massaged into the hair with the fingertips. Rinsing should be done as previously described, and the hair blotted with a towel.

Most men and women need the help that conditioners provide. According to Clairol hair specialists, we can define our hair problems in two dimensions: hereditary characteristics with which we were born, and the condition of the hair as a result of day-to-day living and all the things we do to our hair. Rated from strong to weak, hereditary characteristics are:

Hair holds a set well . . . . Hair does not hold a set
Hair stays put . . . . Hair flies away
Hair is coarse . . . . Hair is fine
Hair has body . . . . Hair lacks body
Hair is thick . . . . Hair is thin

The second dimension, the condition of the hair, refers to characteristics that may result from over-teasing, over-permanenting or -straightening, over-coloring, over–blow drying or over-lightening and from the damaging effects of sun, city soot, salt water, and chlorine water. Rated from good to bad, these attributes are:

Hair isn't too porous . . . . . . Hair is too porous (like a sponge)
Hair rarely has split ends . . . . Hair has split ends
Hair is supple . . . . Hair is brittle
Hair is soft . . . . Hair is dry
Hair has sheen . . . . Hair is dull and drab

No one type of conditioner can eliminate all the problems. Four basic types of hair conditioners are these.

1. *Hairdressings* are used for styling control, hair conditioning, and scalp moisturizing. These are applied directly to the scalp and then combed or brushed through the hair. Once applied, they soften the hair, improve its combability, relieve a dry and itchy scalp, give the hair sheen, and hold the style in place.
2. *Instant conditioners* add sheen, help cure damage, and detangle hair. These are applied after shampooing and are rinsed out after 60 seconds. They work by coating the hair with conditioners and depositing protein that helps fill hair pores.
3. *Body-building conditioners* give body to fine, thin hair. Each strand becomes coated with conditioner and actually increases in diameter. The effect is hair that's fuller and thicker.
4. *Therapeutic or corrective conditioners* help overcome problems related to the condition of the hair. Three primary ingredients penetrate the hair to repair damage: humectants relieve and prevent dryness and add sheen; emollients soften dry, brittle hair; and protein restores natural elasticity and makes hair more supple and resistant to breakage. This "beauty prescription" conditioner helps to correct the balance of oils and protein that keeps hair healthy. This type of conditioner is applied to shampooed, towel-dried hair and left on to work its wonders—about 20–30 minutes for cream forms, and 1–5 minutes for instant lotion forms. Then what has not penetrated the hair shaft is rinsed out.

When hair is really sick, a creme corrective conditioner should be used after each shampoo. When hair is improved, the conditioner should be used two or three times a month. In between, maintain healthy hair with a lotion corrective conditioner.

Other multipurpose hair care products are available that give many of the same conditioning benefits more conveniently, such as creme rinses and conditioning shampoos. It's best to experiment to learn which hair care products keep hair healthy, shining, lustrous, and full of bounce.

If you'd occasionally like to "naturally" enhance the benefits of the many fine shampoos and conditioners that are commercially available, you can whip up your own hair care products at home. Check with your cosmetologist about the suitability of these homemade products for your hair. Here are some "recipes" you might like to try:

Avocado-Egg Conditioner
Beat a room-temperature egg until frothy. Add ½ an avocado that has been pureed until absolutely smooth. The mixture must be perfectly blended before applying to the hair. With a square of cotton, apply to entire scalp; then sponge over the rest of the hair. Massage into scalp. Then cover your head with a towel and leave on for 15 minutes. Add tepid water to hair and work mixture into a lather. Rinse well with warm water until all of the mixture is gone. If you feel any residue in your hair, shampoo gently and rinse again.

Lemon or Vinegar Water Rinse
Mix a tablespoon or two of lemon juice or vinegar in a tall glass of warm water. Pour the rinse over your head, massage in gently, then rinse it out. Follow with a final rinse of warm, clear water.

Hot Oil Treatment
Plain olive, almond, corn, or safflower oil will do. Warm the oil, then section your hair and apply to your entire scalp. Wrap your head in a towel, plastic cap, or old pillowcase. Allow to remain on the scalp for 30 minutes (if hair is very damaged, you might leave it on overnight). Shampoo and rinse very well, until all oil is removed. Before shampooing, you may gently comb the oil through the hair until all ends are coated. Normal hair does not need as long a time before washing out.

Egg Whites
Beat an egg white until frothy, then work into the scalp. Allow to dry; brush out, then shampoo and rinse.

Quick Hints for Highlights:
Blondes
Rinse hair with ½ cup of chamomile flowers brewed with 2 cups of hot water. Grapefruit juice will also work.

Brunettes
Brew rosemary in water, strain, and use this herb water as the final rinse.

A note on drying: Electric dryers are a boon for busy people and are gentle to the hair if used correctly. Most experts recommend using low- or medium-heat settings, keeping the dryer 6–8 inches from your scalp, and using a styling brush to curl or straighten. Keep the dryer moving over your hair to avoid overdrying.

A note on brushing: Select a brush with natural or synthetic bristles that have rounded tips to protect your hair and scalp. A deep brush with long bristles is best for thick hair, while brushes with shorter bristles are good for thin hair. Hair tools for special purposes include the new "vent" brushes (plastic with holes in the base and widely spaced bristles) which add volume by pushing air through your hair; a wooden "rake" for combing curly or wet hair; and spiral brushes to help curl hair as you blowdry. Stiff synthetic-bristled brushes and fine-tooth combs should be avoided because they can damage your hair, especially when it's wet.

As with teeth, there's a right way to brush hair for maximum benefit. Bend over from the waist and brush from back to front. Brush up and out from the scalp, taking each stroke all the way to the hair ends. This will help distribute oil throughout the hair, which is especially important for dry hair. If your hair is curly, brush gently and keep the brush close to your scalp to avoid tangling. If you have any kind of scalp problems, try to brush as little as possible. The old "100 strokes a day" adage is not true for us today! Way back when people did not bathe or wash their hair very often, brushing was the main way to clean the hair. Today, 20 strokes are enough.

Keep your hair brushes and combs clean. Also, since some scalp problems are contagious, you should never lend your brushes and combs to anyone else or borrow another person's. If a brush has broken bristles, throw it away.

CHOOSING A HAIRSTYLE

The right hairstyle can be a work of art—an expression of the unique *you*. Proper styling should achieve balance and harmony with the shape of your face, emphasize good features, camouflage flaws, and adapt to changes in your lifestyle and mood.

The first step toward achieving the right hairstyle is to find a good stylist. These professionals should not only be well-versed in their craft, but should also be interested in designing a style that suits you as an individual. Gone are the days of "carbon copy" hairstyles for men and women. Most of us now want our hair to reflect ourselves, not someone else. Choosing a professional stylist who perceives and understands your needs is essential.

Getting recommendations from friends and associates is a good beginning. You might also try calling a well-known salon and asking for someone who specializes in your hair type. Some stylists prefer working on shorter hair, others on longer hair. Not everyone does everything equally well, so be sure the stylist is adept at working with your hair type and the kind of style you want. (These same principles hold true for having your hair colored, straightened, or permed. Seek out a specialist for these procedures.)

Try out a salon by having a manicure or shampoo and blowdry before committing yourself to anything more serious (and expensive). Ask about prices. Does a single fee cover shampooing, styling, and a blowdry, or is there a lower rate if you've shampooed at home and don't want a blowdry?

If you're pleased with your initial visit to the salon, arrange for a consultation with the stylist you're considering. Bring pictures of hairstyles similar to the one you'd like. Suggest improvements you want to make: playing up your eyes, minimizing protruding ears or a prominent jaw or nose (see Chapters 7 and 8 for specific styling ideas related to these problems). Know what you don't want, as well as what you do. For instance, if you dislike bangs or sideburns, say so. Discuss your lifestyle, leisure activities, usual clothing choices, and the amount of time you are willing to devote to your hair.

Before you agree to a new style, find out how much it will cost to maintain. Also ask what you'll have to do at home to keep the style looking good between appointments.

Don't be intimidated. A good stylist should suggest but not dictate. If you can't talk comfortably with the stylist, or if he or she won't answer your questions and listen to your ideas, you have the wrong person. The stylist should study your face and body proportions before beginning work on your hair. If you think your hair's being cut too short, say, "Stop." If you'd like it even shorter, say so.

Shop for a hairstylist the way you would for any other professional. Your hairstyle is too important to your total appearance to entrust it to a "cutting factory" or to a dictator who won't work with you as an individual.

The descendant of several artists and sculptors, hairstyling expert Peter Hantz emphasizes the importance of understanding the composition of the human face and relating this knowledge to creating the right style for each individual man or woman. He trains other hairstylists in the same way art students are taught. "The human face is divided into thirds: (1) from the chin to the bottom of the nose; (2) from the bottom of the nose to a point just below the eyebrows; (3) from the point just below the eyebrows to the hairline. In the classic oval face, the width is approximately three-fourths the length and the distance between the eyes is the width of one eye."

Of course, few people have perfect oval faces, but Mr. Hantz offers two basic guidelines for achieving the proper balance between hairstyle and any facial shape. They are: (1) Never cut any part of the hair shorter than a measure of the top third of the face. If you have a large forehead, then a short haircut will be quite long. If your forehead is petite, a short haircut will be very short. But either way, the total effect will be one of symmetry. (2) Never cut hair any longer than twice the length of the face. Often, short women think if they wear very long hair, they will look taller. Actually, the reverse is true: the longer the hair, the shorter they look."

A note on hairlines: If your choice of hairstyle is being limited by an uneven or low hairline, you can "clean up" this area permanently with electrolysis. Approximately two to eight hours spread over several visits will be necessary. Fino Gior, President of the International Guild of Professional Electrologists, Inc., describes the procedure: "An almost microscopic filament is inserted into the hair follicle opening, and a very slight amount of heat from a tiny electric current destroys the root. The skin isn't punctured or harmed in any way, and the entire procedure causes very little discomfort, depending on individual sensitivity. Anyone who has ever tweezed or waxed should accept electrolysis very easily." Once your hairline is the shape you desire, you'll only need short touch-up sessions to remove new hair growth during the next two years. After that, regrowth should stop.

Before

After

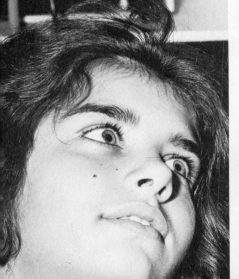
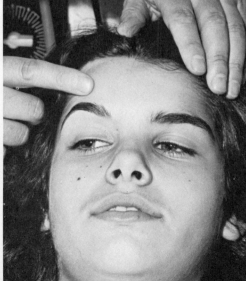

Victoria Principal   Polly Bergen

STYLING BASICS: WOMEN

In addition to finding a style that balances the shape of your face, you'll also need to consider your lifestyle. If you're a banker or lawyer, you'll need a different look than a high-fashion model. If you prefer tailored, classic clothes to fluffy dresses or blouses, your hairstyle should reflect these indications of your personality. You'll also want a style that fits into your schedule. Most people today want easy care, as well as a great look! Among the well-known women who have influenced hairstyles are those pictured above.

Here are some guidelines for the six basic facial configurations:

Oval — This shape is considered the model for all other shapes to achieve, since so many lengths, styles, and looks are attractive on the classic oval. Like having normal skin and hair—you're lucky to have an oval face. Enjoy!

Round — To slim the face and add planes for contrast, try soft, narrowing lines; avoid pulling hair straight back or any "boxy" styles. Unless you have a high forehead, avoid straight, long bangs.

Square/Rectangular — To minimize angular features and broad lines in a *square* face, use styles that add softness and roundness at the temples and jaw-line. Avoid haircuts shorter than chin-length, boxy styles, or too much hair on the face. The *rectangular* face may be softened with fullness at the cheekbones, rounded edges at the temples, and chin-line and chin-length cuts.

Diamond — Try to add fullness at the points (temples and chin), and keep hair hugging the head at the widest area (the cheekbones). Avoid center parts and severe, off-the-face styles.

Pear — To minimize the broad jawline and make it balance with a narrow forehead, add volume at the top and bangs for length. If your hair is very limp, a body wave or perm might help. Avoid center parts and very long hair.

Heart (inverted triangle) — Too much width at the forehead and a pointy chin can be minimized with layered cuts that give length to the crown and width to the chin. Avoid severe styles and very short haircuts.

STYLING BASICS: MEN

Modern men have increased freedom in choosing hairstyles. While men don't enjoy as many options as women, there's plenty of room for individuality instead of simply "taking a little off the top." Also, it's no longer unusual for men to color, straighten, or curl their hair. Some men's styling makeovers are shown below.

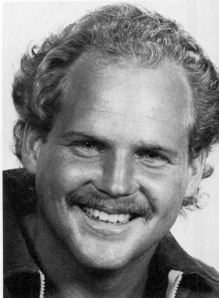

Before   After

Before

After

Before

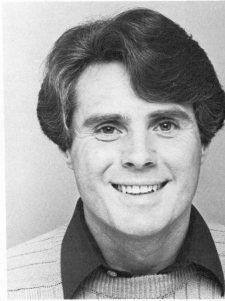

After

Your hairstyle should be functional and easy for you to maintain at home. A style may look perfect the day it's done, but you may never again achieve the same look. Let the stylist know if you're adept with a blow dryer—or all thumbs. It can make a difference in the style he or she provides.

Your hairstyle is your most important asset in minimizing flaws and emphasizing good features. If you are blessed with terrific bone structure, a style that opens up your face will flatter your good features. But what if your ears are too large? Your nose is too prominent? Your chin recedes? The length and fullness of your hair plus the angle of the cut can effectively correct these problems.

Whatever your occupation—from coach to corporation president —your career and leisure activities will influence your choice of hairstyle. If most of your clothing is conservative and you spend a lot of time among conservative people, you may need to stick to a simple style and forgo a moustache or beard. Actors, musicians, and college professors may have more leeway in choosing styles. The most important factors are being comfortable with the style and feeling good about the way you look.

As with women, your facial shape is critical to your hairstyle. Here are guidelines for the six classic groupings:

Oval — Almost any style will flatter an oval face. Choose one that doesn't resist your hair type and accents your facial shape and features.

Round — Round faces need definition. Wear a short style with a side part, if you can, to offset the roundness.

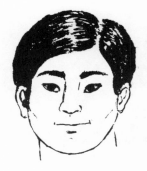

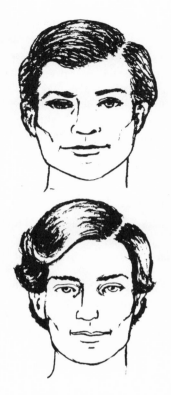

Square/Rectangular — With a *square* face, try short styles and side parts to "round off" any harsh angles and add length. With the *rectangular* face—long lines and sharp angles—adding height at the crown and fullness at the sides will reduce the appearance of length.

Diamond — You may be able to wear longer styles well. A center part will add length and draw attention up from the widest area at the cheekbones.

Pear — Emphasize hair at the crown to balance a broad jawline. Wear styles off the forehead to add width. Avoid long styles and center parts.

Heart (inverted triangle) — Styles that add fullness to the jawline minimize a pointy chin; a side part will cut width at the crown. Try medium-length cuts to emphasize your eyes. You might also consider a moustache to strengthen your jawline.

CHANGING STRAIGHTNESS OR CURLINESS

Unless completely out of control, your naturally curly or straight hair should work for you with the right styling cut. However, if you don't like your hair the way it is—or have difficulty caring for it, despite the cut—there are alternatives.

First are the nonpermanent solutions. For adding curl to straight hair, you can choose between setting your hair on rollers or producing temporary curls with an electric hairsetter or curling wand. Thermal straightening (or pressing) involves the use of a curling wand to temporarily relax tightly curled hair into looser curls. Clairol specialists say any of these procedures may be used immediately following a hair color application.

Permanent solutions to the straight- or curly-hair problem produce changes that will last until new hair grows in. For straight hair, permanents or cold waves are the choice. These have come a long way since the time when early waving processes resulted in corkscrew curls and damaged hair. A protein-splitting chemical called ammonium thioglycolate is used to chemically alter the hair fiber. For a tight curl, thin curler rods are used; for a looser "body" wave, larger rods are applied.

Peter Hantz has devised a two-step process that combines both ideas—first applying a smaller rod and "separating the hair into segments with a tremendous capacity to curl," then replacing the smaller rods with larger curlers angled to achieve the maximum control over the direction in which the hair falls. Called "restructuring," this technique makes it possible for men and women to have more choice in their style, says Mr. Hantz. "They can comb the restructured hair back into a straight style or ruffle it with their fingers for a curly look. And, it's ideal for controlling cowlicks or unruly hair that keeps flopping down on your forehead."

Hair straighteners or relaxers also are chemicals that change the configuration of the hair. They transform small, tight, natural curls into larger and smoother curls—a process often sought by Black men and women. The three types of relaxing agents generally used are: (1) sodium hydroxide, an alkali that is the most effective but is also the most damaging to the hair; (2) thioglycolate, which is less damaging; and (3) sodium bisulfite, the newest process, which is almost as effective as the alkalies and much safer. Chemical straight-

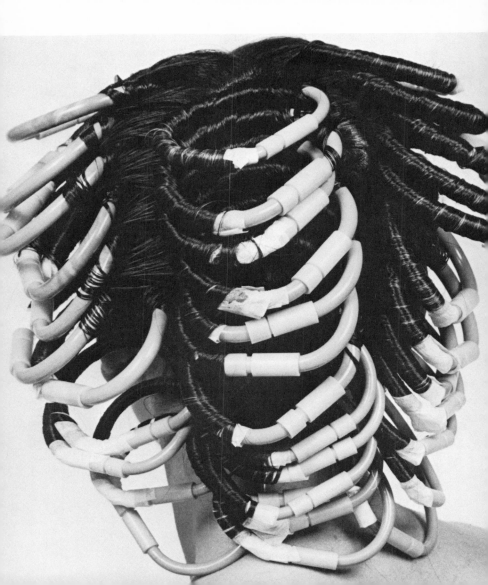

eners should not be used immediately after hair coloring, according to Clairol experts. They recommend a waiting period of seven to ten days between the two processes.

Hair waving and straightening procedures may be done by a professional cosmetologist or by you at home. If you decide to "do it yourself," however, do read and follow instructions very carefully.

COLOR CONSIDERATIONS

Should you or shouldn't you? For men as well as women, changing the color of your hair is an important decision. It can give you a lift, make you feel and look younger, update your fashion image.

When Clairol and *The Ladies' Home Journal* asked readers to tell them how hair coloring had changed their lives,[34] the responses included the following comments:

- "I not only found myself more attractive and beautiful, but I found myself a career."
- "I look ten years younger. I know it. I've been told many times. I am a new person."
- "I had to admit that it certainly does make me feel different inside. I lost a few pounds, got a terrific tan to show off my hair, bought new clothes in colors to compliment my new hair color. I'm having a ball."
- "I used to be so shy in my work, but now I have the confidence to speak up in business meetings, which has helped boost my position from payroll clerk to executive secretary and bookkeeper."
- "The hair color change was such an improvement that it gave me more self-confidence. It gave me the courage to dress up to it with more youthful and colorful clothes. Soon, the promotion and raise in salary, which I had given up on because raises and promotions seemed to go to the younger employees, became a reality for me!"
- "My temperament is that of a redhead. I've always longed to be a redhead and have that special pizzazz. Now I feel like the real me."

If you decide a major color change is called for, consult a trusted professional. Learn the options; find out what to look (and look out) for. In addition to a total color change, you may want to investigate procedures for frosting, streaking, or tipping your hair— all of which change the color of selected strands for a more dramatic or highlighted effect.

Celebrated beauty authority Leslie Blanchard says you can create illusions with your hair color, just as you do with your hairstyle.

Used correctly, color can work wonders in flattering your face. Just remember this general rule of thumb that he advises: warm hair colors, those with reddish or golden undertones, are advancing colors. They seem to bring things (in this case, your face) closer, emphasizing them and making them appear more important. The ashen hair colors, those with no reddish or golden undertones, are receding colors. They seem to make things look farther away, minimizing them so they seem smaller or camouflaged.

The use of hair coloring products by men has become increasingly common, according to Mr. Hantz. The major reason men turn to hair coloring is to cover or lessen the intensity of gray hair. "On many men, there is nothing more attractive than gray hair," he says. "But a heavier man especially, or one who has a round face, needs some framing in order to halt the expansion of the facial line. Even a man like Johnny Carson would benefit from a bit of color with his gray hair. The hair needn't be totally colored. By going out about an inch from the hairline to begin the tinting, the outgrowth wouldn't be apparent and his face would be nicely framed."

Both men and women should stay close to their original adult hair coloring. Trying to revert to the shades of youth is a mistake because our complexions change as we get older. Blondes may have more fun, but the towhead that looked great as a kid appears ridiculous at 45. Using the charts on pages 99–100, consider what hair colors might be right for you. Then, to get an idea of how they'll look on you, try on a few wigs in the color (or colors) you're contemplating.

There are three basic categories of hair coloring products:

1. *Temporary* products do not change the color of the hair shaft; they are usually rinsed in and wash out with the next shampoo. Men and women use temporary colors to add highlights to their own color, tone down brassiness, or remove yellow tones from gray hair.

2. *Semi-permanent* hair colors do penetrate the hair shaft, but do not significantly change the color. They usually last for three to five washings before fading. They will cover or blend in gray hairs, bring out highlights in hair and enhance natural shades.

3. *Permanent* hair coloring products actually change the pigment of the hair shaft with peroxide. They can't be washed out, but must grow out with the hair. They offer the greatest range of shade difference, can lighten or darken natural shades, and completely cover gray.

To go from a dark shade to a pale blonde, you'll need a double process: stripping the dark shade from the hair shafts, then toning the hair to the shade you want. This can be a tricky process, so if you're doing your own coloring, be sure to follow instructions very carefully.

With all of these procedures, a patch test (for scalp sensitivity) and strand test (to check color change) should be done beforehand. With patience and practice, all of these coloring procedures may be done as effectively at home as by a professional.

A note on Black hair: Black men and women need specially designed hair coloring products with plenty of conditioning benefit. Clairol specialists warn that Black hair can be weakened by popular styling techniques like chemical straightening, thermal pressing, and picking. These weakening techniques, plus the unique curl pattern of Black hair, can result in excessive breakage and dryness.

WIGS AND HAIRPIECES

For women, wigs and hairpieces generally are an accessory—a means of maintaining a terrific-looking hairstyle at all times or of adding a little extra pizzazz to their normal hair arrangement. For men, the decision to buy a wig or hairpiece results from a balding (or bald) pate.

In either case, Josef of Rome, noted wig designer and Vice President of Eva Gabor International, offers some general guidelines for selecting a wig or hairpiece:

1. Wigs and hairpieces are available in both natural hair (quite expensive) and synthetic fibers (very reasonably priced).
2. Color is the major consideration. For a hairpiece, the color should match as closely as possible the man or woman's natural hair shade. A wig also should be close to the natural color, although more leeway is possible here, as long as the color is compatible with a person's skin tones.
3. Styling is the next important point. This should conform to the same rules as those for styling your natural hair: to balance the shape of your face and your features. Among the trendsetters who have inspired wig designs are First Lady Nancy Reagan and Diana, Princess of Wales.
4. When buying a wig, try on at least four or five styles and shades to be sure you're getting the one that's best for you. What looks good on someone else at the wig counter or in the salon may not be right for you.

SKIN TYPES AND SUGGESTED HAIR COLORS

SKIN TYPE:	VERY PALE	PALE AND ROSY
Special Advice	Make skin warmer with golden hair color: avoid ashy and very pale blonde shades.	Tone down pink skin with ashy, subdued hair color.
Best Color Choices	• Light golden to honey blondes • Reddish blonde to golden auburn • Light to deep golden browns • Deep brunette (if natural hair color is dark)	• Pale to ashy blondes • Light to medium ash browns • Muted auburns
SALLOW	FLORID	BLACK
Brighten olive or yellow skin with lighter, brighter hair color; avoid drab ashy colors and pale blonde shades.	Tone down reddish skin with ashen hair color; avoid too red a color.	The darker the skin, the deeper and warmer the hair color should be; avoid ashy shades.
• Dark golden blonde • Light to dark golden browns • Deep, rich brunette	• Sandy to ash blonde • Light to medium ash browns • Muted auburn	• Soft auburn • Rich golden browns • Burgundy browns

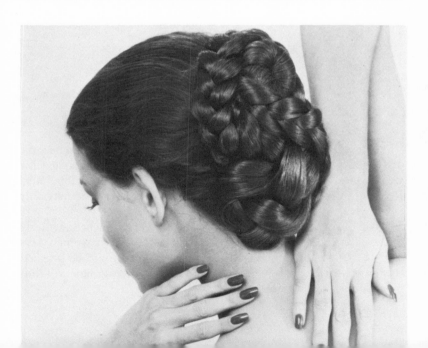

WAYS OF CHANGING HAIR COLOR

COLOR CHANGE	WHAT YOU NEED
For sunny highlights	A Special Effects Kit • Lighten selected strands of hair • Highlight a little around face; or highlight more throughout hair • Recommended for light brown to blonde hair
To make your own color more attractive without changing it	A Non-peroxide Hair Coloring • Brightens your own color • Covers gray • Adds highlights • Washes out after a few shampoos • Will not lighten or change natural hair color
To make your hair color lighter or darker	A One-Step Shampoo Formula Hair Coloring • Go lighter • Go darker • Enrich your own hair color • Shampoos in; takes about 20 minutes • Color lasts until hair grows out • Reapply color about once a month
To go very blonde	A Two-Step Blonding Kit • To go pale blonde if hair is fairly dark or has red undertones • Use lightener kit to remove dark color from hair • Use toner kit to put in blonde shade of your choice
To make gray hair more attractive	A Gray Enhancer • Minimizes yellow tones • Evens out gray • Non-peroxide; washes out after a few shampoos

The major problem with men's hairpieces is that they can become dislodged at embarrassing moments; however, styles designed for wear while swimming or in the shower are now available. Burt Reynolds, Frank Sinatra, Tony Bennett, and Michael Landon readily acknowledge their use of well-designed hairpieces.

Like normal hair, wigs and hairpieces should be washed regularly and kept in good condition. A common mistake among women, says Mr. Josef, is failure to brush their wigs. "They should be brushed thoroughly or be slightly teased at the base so the wig hair will fluff out and appear more natural."

Wig style inspired by Nancy Reagan

Mr. Hantz offers another solution for men who are partially bald. "One of my clients who has a monk's rim–type receding hairline let his hair grow quite long; then he permed it and pulled it forward, cutting it to resemble the natural hairline; and then used surgical glue to attach the hair to the bald area. I have a very critical eye and I couldn't detect what he'd done," Mr. Hantz relates. Since then the hair specialist has successfully used this procedure, along with his "restructuring" process, to provide other men with their own natural hairpiece.

"The results of this technique in no way resemble the awful effect created by so many men, who try to hide their balding hairline by combing a few strands of hair from one side across the balding area," he cautions. "The attempt at artifice is obvious in those cases because the horizontal sweep of the longer hair doesn't look like a normal hairline. But with the back-to-front procedure, you have a very natural appearance."

HAIR-REPLACEMENT TECHNIQUES

Hair loss is one of the most difficult and upsetting problems involving hair and appearance. So far, no one has discovered an elixir, potion, or magic formula that will prevent hair loss or restore hair once it's gone. Here are the factors involved:

1. *Bleaching/permanents/straightening.* When done badly or too often, these techniques may cause hair breakage and loss. The hair will usually grow back, as long as you discontinue the source of the damage.
2. *Teasing/ponytails/too-tight hairstyles.* These may cause so much tension that the follicles become damaged and hair loss results. Try to avoid these styles and methods—or use them judiciously.
3. *Illness/injury/certain drugs/X-ray therapy/birth control pills/pregnancy.* Any of these can contribute to hair loss. Be sure you know the side effects of every drug you take, and discuss abnormal hair loss with your doctor. If the dosage or type of drug can't be altered, you may need to sacrifice some hair to get well. Many times, it will grow back.
4. *Alopecia areata.* This is a patchy baldness for which there is no known cause or real cure (sometimes cortisone helps). At times this condition is permanent; however, it also can reverse itself spontaneously.

Permanent hair loss is primarily the result of the aging process and common (or "male-pattern") baldness. While actors Yul Brynner and Telly Savalas have turned their glowing, hair-free heads into part of their sex appeal and newsmen Charles Kuralt and Irving R. Levine have distinguished themselves on television despite conspicuous lack of hair, most men still feel that balding detracts from their appearance.

With the passage of time, hair thins and recedes, an experience shared by both men and women, although most pronounced in men. The loss is usually gradual and slight enough that many people decide they can live with the situation.

Common baldness is an inherited genetic trait that causes men to bald in a predictable pattern that cannot be stopped or reversed. As

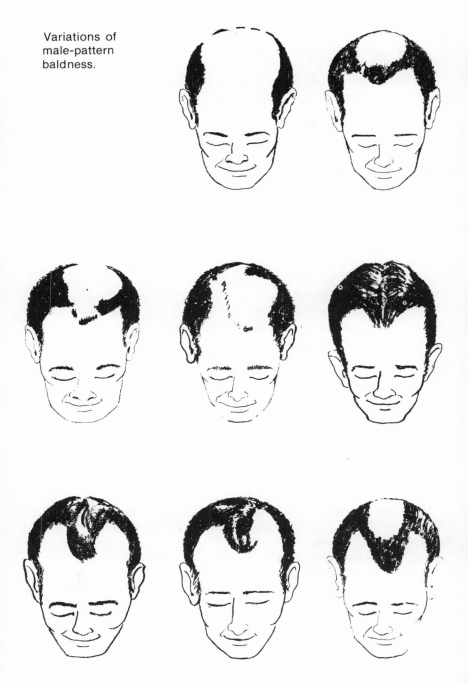

Variations of male-pattern baldness.

shown on page 103, eight balding patterns have been identified. They range from little hair loss to the most severe, eventual total baldness.

This condition can begin at a relatively young age and seems to stem from the effects of the male hormone androgen, which both men and women possess to varying degrees. Hormone treatments do not, however, seem to correct the problem. Ongoing research has thus far produced no positive results.

In addition to the use of wigs and hairpieces, several replacement techniques offer solace to many balding individuals.

The three hair-replacement techniques used most often today are hair weaving, implants, and transplants. All have advantages and disadvantages—and all three areas are ripe for exploitation by quacks. Choosing a procedure is a highly personal decision and requires careful investigation. No one can work miracles and "restore hair to life." Be very wary: check with doctors, talk to friends, call the Better Business Bureau.

In very simplified terms, *hair weaving* and *hair implants* are methods of securing a hairpiece to your scalp. As a rule, these procedures are done in "clinics" rather than by physicians, so you should be as knowledgeable as possible before going for a consultation. With hair weaving an anchor is formed from your own hair for a hairpiece. Hair implants involve the use of sutures or wire anchors implanted in your scalp and attached to the hairpiece.

Hair transplants should only be performed by qualified plastic surgeons or dermatologists. Brought to national attention by Senator William Proxmire and television host Hugh Downs, hair transplanting involves the following steps: (1) Hair plugs or strips are removed from areas of the scalp (usually the back or sides) where hair growth is normal; (2) Approximately 30 to 70 of these plugs are then grafted in a predetermined pattern to the bald scalp. Because these are from your own body, they won't be rejected as a foreign body would be; (3) Several procedures are necessary to achieve an aesthetically pleasing result.

Not everyone is a suitable candidate for a hair transplant; however, those who do undergo this procedure seem to be pleased with the finished product. For example, one of my patients was a college senior whose luxuriant red beard and moustache were offset by a largely bald head. As this condition progressed, he changed from an outgoing and active young man to a loner who thought about dropping out of school. Following transplant surgery, he completed his education and is now happily engaged in his chosen career field.

1.

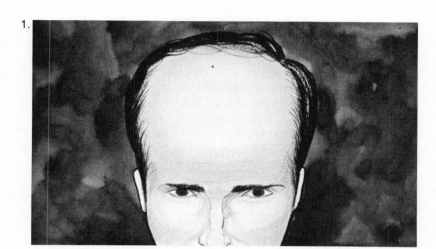

2.

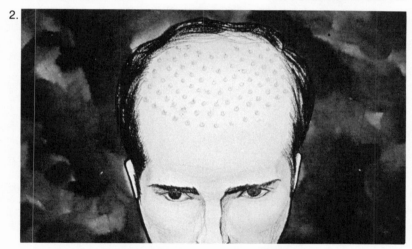

3.

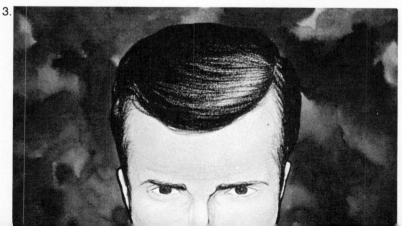

Because one of the major challenges in hair-transplant surgery is to create a natural-looking hairline, I've worked with a local hair-stylist in deciding on the best placement of the donor plugs. One of the cases with which the stylist assisted me involved a middle-aged real estate broker who was constantly in touch with the public. His self-image was that the hair loss he had experienced following a heart attack and open heart surgery made him look ten years older than his actual age. After his hair-transplant surgeries were completed, he expressed his feelings in this way: "Having hair on my head again gives me a lift. My energy's back, and I feel and look good. It's restored the way I feel about myself as a person—and what's more, if I ever decide I need a face lift, I'm going to have one!"

6

FROM THE TOP

**"If I could write the beauty of your eyes
And in fresh numbers number all your graces,
The age to come would say, 'This poet lies;
Such heavenly touches ne'er touched earthly
faces.'"**[35]

The "winsome eye" and "unfettered brow" have drawn the attention of poets, playwrights, songwriters, and authors through the ages. Like them, most of us are drawn to people not only by an attractive appearance and good grooming, but by the open, animated expressions of thoughts and emotions displayed in the upper reaches of the face.

Some well-known people have very identifiable eyes. As part of its campaign to encourage all of us to take better care of our eyes, the American Optometric Association devised the "Most Distinctive Eyes" Award. Those selected were: Mikhail Baryshnikov, Carol Channing, Bette Davis, Goldie Hawn, Liza Minnelli, Suzanne Pleshette, Jane Seymour, Omar Sharif, Brooke Shields, and Elizabeth Taylor.

Our eyes reveal a great deal about our energy, personality, and outlook—and play a significant part in first impressions. They also are particularly vulnerable to the effects of aging, poor nutrition, and neglect, which can dull their gleam and detract from the positive image we'd like to convey to others.

Inadequate lighting or untreated vision problems lead to furrowed brows, frowning, and squinting, which take a heavy toll on the delicate skin around the eyes and may eventually cause deep creases in the forehead, brow, and eye areas.

Fortunately, however, our eyes readily respond to proper care. Nature provides many protective measures, but we must take time to preserve and protect these important aspects of our appearance from injury and disease.

The skin surrounding the eye is highly vulnerable to the effects of stress and aging. Because the skin in the eye area is so very delicate, it tends to wrinkle more easily. Also, this area is fed by only a few small oil glands, so the skin tends to be drier, burns more quickly than other areas, and is more susceptible to the ravages of heat, cold, wind, sun, and pollution. To care for these tissues and help preserve sparkling eyes, here are some recommended basics to add to your health or beauty regimen:

1. Always protect the eyes from sunlight, sunlamps, or other tanning rays. Use sunscreens or sun-blocks, and glasses or goggles. Moisturize often.

2. Pat the eye area dry after cleansing. Never rub your eyes, and don't pull the skin when applying makeup. Also, use gentle strokes inward when applying creams, cleansers, or oils.

3. Fluids tend to collect in the face, especially the eyes and cheeks, overnight. If you awaken with puffy eyes, try sleeping on your back or side and use a plump pillow. To avoid wrinkles and creases, sleep with your face turned away from the pillow. These "wake-up creases" are only temporary now, but years of repeated furrowing and bunching of facial skin may make them permanent.

4. Sleep in a darkened room or wear a sleep mask to keep eyes from straining against the light. Use an under-eye cream daily, and reapply often in harsh weather.

5. For head and eye discomforts—including tired, puffy or swollen eyes, tension headaches, and hangovers—relax and strap on a liquid- or gel-filled goggle-like eye mask that has been chilled in the refrigerator or freezer. Herb masks and cotton balls or gauze pads soaked in strong solutions of cold mint or chamomile tea also make wonderful balms for sore eyes, as do cold cucumber slices. Place on each eye and lie down for about 15 minutes.

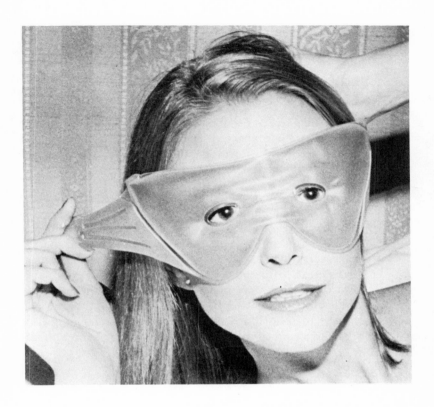

6. The French have a special routine for dealing with bags under the eyes. First, using your index fingers, press firmly against the bridge of the nose for five seconds. Then repeat this procedure on the inside corners, the edge of the eye socket bone, and along the socket to the temples and, finally, your hairline.

7. Smoking has been linked to the occurrence of "crow's feet"— those tiny lines at the corners of the eyes. If you smoke, this may provide another good reason to stop.

8. Try to become aware of how much you frown, squint, crinkle your eyes, grimace, and contort your face, Naturally, you don't want to become an expressionless automaton. However, we often abuse facial skin with unnecessary frowning. If you have difficulty seeing, have your eyes checked!

9. If the whites of your eyes aren't as clear as they should be, try increasing your intake of water (not other beverages), since the cause may be insufficient moisture. Another source may be hereditary: melanin deposits cause reddish or brownish spots in the eyes of many Blacks.

10. "Road map" eyes resulting from lack of sleep, too much alcohol, or environmental irritation can be helped with the use of eyedrops. However, eliminating the source of the problem is the best solution.

11. Both men and women should protect the skin around the eyes by regular application of moisturizing creams specifically designed for use around the eyes. (These are lighter in texture than regular facial moisturizers because of the eye skin's very thin texture.) Apply a small amount of moisturizer next to the nose on the upper lid and gently pat it toward the outer corner and then underneath the eye to the bridge of the nose. After 20 minutes, gently pat the area with a tissue to absorb any excess moisturizer remaining (this won't be absorbed and will interfere with makeup application).

FRAMING THE EYES

Since the brows frame the eyes, proper shaping is important for the most attractive appearance. First, you must find the shape that is natural for your eyes. Your brows should begin at the inside corner of the eye, arch at the edge of the iris, and end about one-fourth inch from the outer edge of the eye. You can use your eyebrow pencil to find the correct parameters for your eyes:

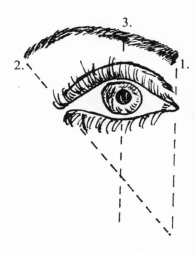

1. Hold the pencil straight up from the outer edge of your nose to the inner corner of the eye. Where the point falls, make a dot.

2. Form a diagonal line from the base of the nose to the outer rim of the iris and place a dot at the point where the pencil touches your brow.

3. Slide the pencil to the edge of the eye socket bone and make a dot where the inner edge of the pencil falls.

4. The dots indicate where your eyebrows should begin and end and the highest point of the arch. Now, tweeze away excess or straggly hairs from around the brow. To reduce discomfort, tweeze in the direction of hair growth.
   Note: Men or women with bushy eyebrows or eyebrows that extend across the bridge of the nose often feel they'll look more attractive if some of the excess hairs are removed.

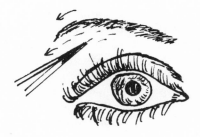

5. If eyebrows are too short or thin, use a pencil to sketch in tiny hairs, making feathery strokes and smudging the edges for a realistic appearance. To lift the eyes, brush your brows up and out.

6. Brows should be one or two shades lighter than hair color, if not the same shade. An exception is blondes, who should go a shade darker. *Avoid black.* Also, eyebrows can be professionally tinted or dyed for better definition. Both men and women find this a simple and effective procedure.

7. If you wear eyeglasses, strive for naturalness and a clean line. Avoid bushiness or tweezing the brows in an overly arched manner so that they compete with your frames. Ideally, the top rims of your frames should cover your eyebrows. Otherwise, you may appear to have two sets of eyebrows.

In addition to tweezing, men and women have several other choices for removing unwanted eyebrow hair. A nonpermanent method is waxing, which removes hair from the roots. You'll probably want to have this done by a professional esthetician. Hot wax is applied to the area where hair is to be removed; allowed to harden; then pulled off, bringing out the hairs with it.

Another choice that permanently removes facial hair is electrolysis, a procedure described in the preceding chapter. This technique is frequently selected for the elimination of unwanted hair around and between the eyebrows. It takes several visits, totaling an estimated two to six hours of electrolysis.

Caution: For eyebrows, never use a razor to remove hair, unless you don't mind the unsightly stubble that will eventually result.

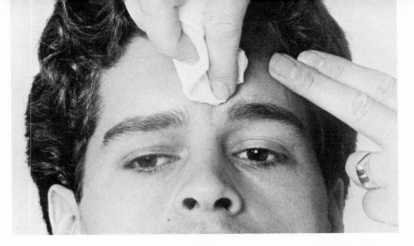

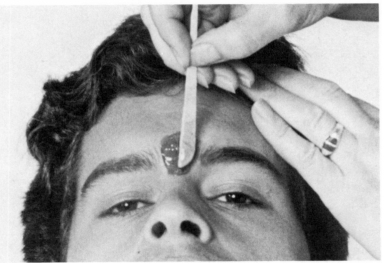

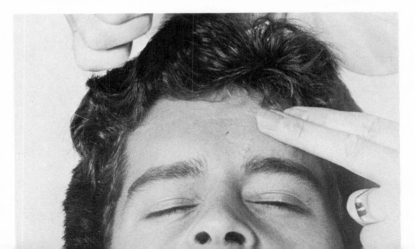

EYE MAKEUP

As most of us know, the cosmetic arts can accomplish amazing transformations, especially in creating alluring eyes. If you use foundation on the rest of your face, apply it also around your eyes. Next, apply eye shadows (in cream, liquid, crayon, or powder form) with a brush or sponge applicator. Avoid bright blues and turquoise eye shadows and white highlighter—they're too harsh for almost everyone. The idea is to enhance your eyes, not the lids. (See chart on page 119 for best color selections.) The basic steps for eye makeup are:

1. *Color the lid.* Choose a color that harmonizes with your eyes and clothing.

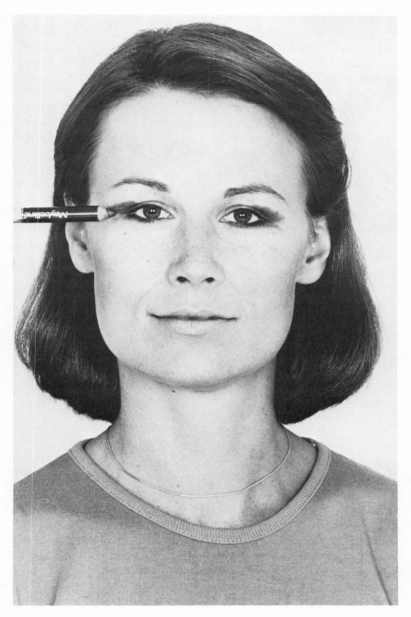

2. *Apply contour.* Use a deep shade of shadow and blend it upward and outward to define the eye. Apply just above the natural crease.

3. *Apply highlighter.* Use the lightest shade to bring eyes forward.
Apply under the brow on the browbone, and blend outward.

4. *Apply liner*. If you use liner at all, apply it in a thin line to give lashes a base. Smudge with a cotton swab or sponge applicator to soften the line.

5. *Apply mascara.* Dark brown, blue-black, or black works for every eye color. Mascara will do the most to dramatize eyes, so use two or three coats. Start at the inner corner and brush up and out, concentrating on the outer lashes to add length to eye shape. Apply a coat to the lower lashes and then brush the underside of the top lashes. Allow each coat to dry before applying the next.

Eye makeup always should be removed before going to sleep. Use cleansing cream, mineral oil, or eye makeup remover on a cotton ball to gently wipe off shadow, liner, and waterproof mascara. Soap and water will remove cake mascara, and conditioning or lash-building mascara requires a non-oily remover. When taking off mascara, close your eyes over a tissue and gently wipe the lashes in a downward motion.

Additional notes about eyelashes: To curl or not to curl—that is the question many women debate. Some people believe that using an eyelash curler accelerates the normal rate at which your eyelashes fall out. If you do want to curl your lashes to make your eyes appear larger, experts advise that you do so with a series of gentle squeezes rather than clamping the curler onto the lashes for a minute or more.

GUIDE TO SELECTING EYE MAKEUP COLORS*

EYE COLOR	EYE SHADOW	SHADING	HIGHLIGHTS	LINER AND MASCARA
Light, medium deep blue, or violet	Brown Blue Violet Mauve	Brown Navy Green Charcoal	Ivory White Pale yellow Pale pink	Black Charcoal Brown Navy
Blue-green	Grey Navy		Beige	Dark green Bright blue
Blue-gray	Silver Gold			Silver Gold
Green	Turquoise	Brown	Ivory	Black or charcoal
Hazel	Green			Dark brown
Brown	Brown	Green	Peach Light pink	Dark blue or navy
Dark brown	Mauve	Navy	Light yellow	Dark green
Black	Taupe Gold	Charcoal	Beige Silver	Silver Gold

NOTE: The makeup artist will experiment with color combinations to achieve the desired results. Generally colors of the same color family are used for a more natural look. For example, brown eye shadow, shaded with a deeper brown, highlighted with beige will create a pleasant contrast. Dark brown liner and mascara will further enhance this combination of basic colors. Startling color contrasts are usually preferred for evening.

* The above chart by permission of the Milady Publishing Corporation, from the Standard Textbook for Professional Estheticians.

In addition to the use of mascara, eyelashes can be professionally tinted or dyed for long-lasting (about three to four weeks), smudge-proof color. This process takes about 30 minutes and is particularly advantageous for men and women whose lashes are light.

False eyelashes have primarily been used by entertainers to make their eyes look larger and more appealing. A variety of styles are available, and if you're considering this cosmetic adjunct, you may want to consult a professional esthetician about choosing the best style for you and learning how to apply and care for your false eyelashes. Basically, your lashes should be applied before eye makeup is added. A glue (such as surgical adhesive, which is available in most drugstores) is stroked along the base of your natural lashes with a toothpick or eyeliner brush. Then the false eyelashes are pressed into position. They'll remain in place for about a week. Non-oily makeup and makeup remover should be used with false eyelashes. Mascara isn't recommended since it can't be taken off without removing the lashes as well.

A more popular, natural-looking choice is to have a professional esthetician fill out your eyelashes by attaching individual false lashes directly to your natural eyelashes. These will remain in place until the lashes to which they are attached fall out—from a few days to several weeks.

CORRECTING PROBLEMS FOR DIFFERENT EYE TYPES

Here are some suggestions for using makeup to make the most of some common eye-type problems. To become more adept at applying any of the techniques described, you can practice on the eye drawings on page 127. Work with the pencils and the colors you will be using on your eyes.

1. *Drooping lids.* Line the outer curve of the lower lid and extend the line upward. Apply translucent color on the upper lid above the crease. Keep colors simple.

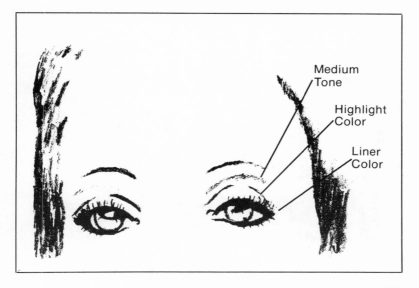

2. *Close-set eyes*. Use pale shadow on the inner half of the lid, a medium shade on the outer half. Line only the outer curve of the lid.

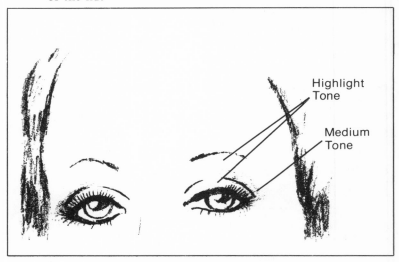

Highlight Tone

Medium Tone

3. *Deep-set eyes*. Apply a neutral shade to the inner corner; a light shade on the lid to bring the eye forward; and a bright shade in the crease.

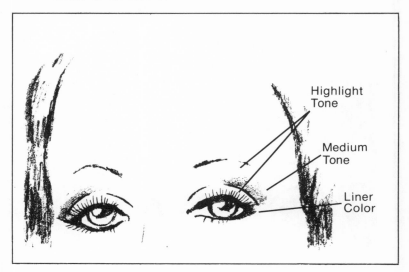

Highlight Tone

Medium Tone

Liner Color

4. *Small eyes.* Sweep color out to the side, along the eye bone, and under the bottom lashes.

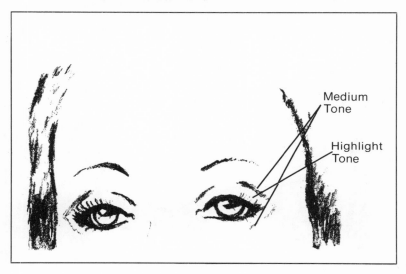

5. *Aging eyelids.* Use soft, natural tones of creamy shadow. Contour the folds over the brow bone. Use very little liner, if any, and smudge the edges. Use nonsmear mascara to really play up your eyes, rather than garish colors and eyeliner.

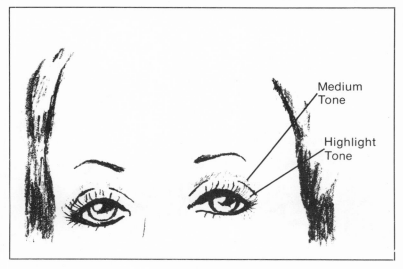

6. *Wide-set eyes*. Line the inside of the lower lid with bright color. Highlight the center of the lid with pale shadow.

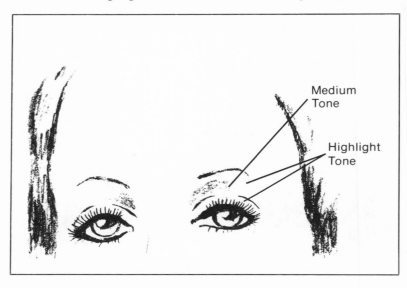

7. *Protruding eyes*. Line the upper and lower lids with dark color; use a deep tone of shadow on the upper lids; highlight the brow bone.

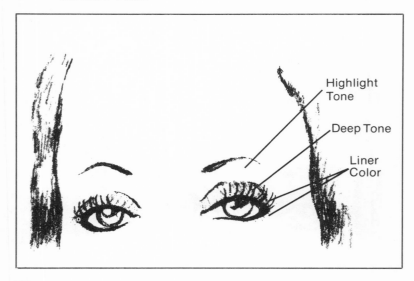

8. *Oriental eyes.* Blend white shadow over the entire lid. Contour the eye socket with a deep tone of shadow, using a slight upward slant at the outer edge.

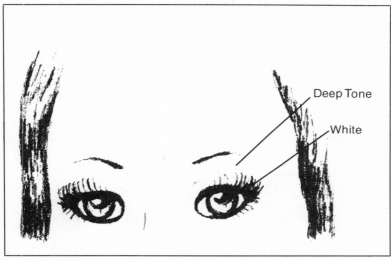

Deep Tone

White

9. *Wrinkles/crow's feet.* Fill in lines with foundation or bronzer a shade lighter than the skin tone, using a small brush. Use a light, cream-base under-eye makeup. Add cream shadows (powder shadow tends to collect in wrinkles) in soft hues. Keep colors light and edges smudged for a soft look.

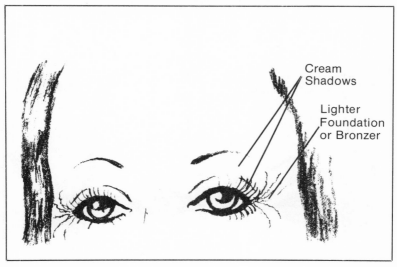

Cream Shadows

Lighter Foundation or Bronzer

10. *Dark shadows under eyes.* Hide by applying makeup cover stick, bronzer, or foundation a shade lighter than your natural coloring. Use a small brush and apply only to dark areas, not to the entire under-eye region. Then add regular foundation all over. (*Do not* use powder underneath the eyes; it will further dehydrate an area already short of moisture.)

Lighter Foundation or Bronzer

11. *Bags under eyes.* Apply makeup cover stick, bronzer, or foundation a shade darker than your natural coloring to make bags recede; then add regular foundation all over.

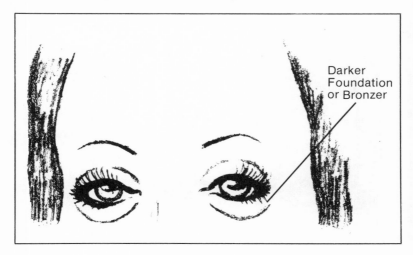

Darker Foundation or Bronzer

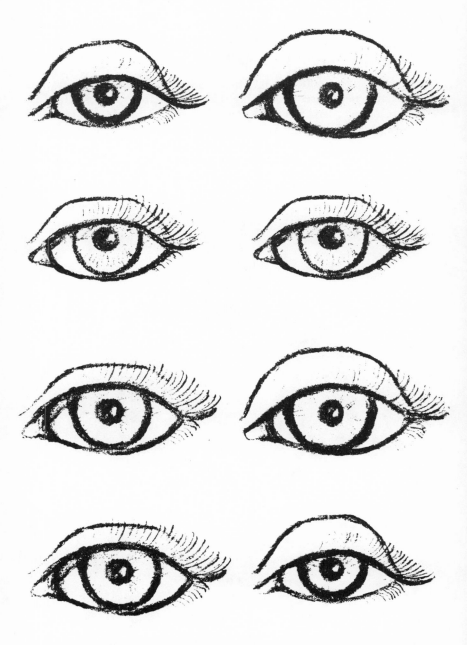

Practice contouring and highlighting for your eyes on these drawings
—use colored pencils in shades similar to those you'll use on your own
eyes.

SPECIAL TIPS FOR EYEGLASS AND CONTACT LENS WEARERS

If you wear soft contact lenses, insert them prior to applying makeup; hard lenses may be inserted either before or after makeup. Also, contact lens wearers should not use lash-building mascara, since particles sometimes flake off and can irritate the eyes.

Women who wear eyeglasses need to use their eye makeup for special emphasis, so their eyes won't be hidden by the glasses. Here are some basic eye-makeup tips for eyeglass wearers from the Optical Manufacturers Association:

1. Start with a concealing cream or stick around the entire eye area, concentrating under the eye. This will make the eyes look larger.

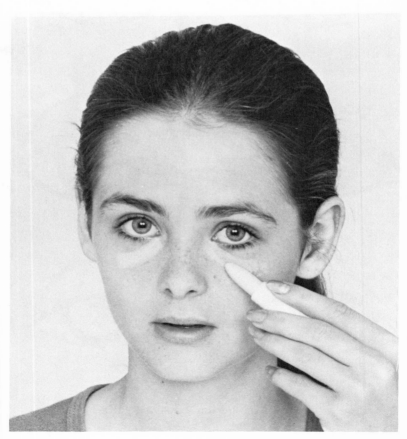

2. Shade the brow-bone area with a dark eye shadow. With a lighter shade, fill in the lid itself, to help draw the eyes forward and make them look larger. Keep the color deepest at the outer corners, gradually blending it outward from the center.
3. Brush on a lot of mascara for the longest, thickest lashes possible. Use heavy mascara especially on the lower lashes to accentuate this area. Also, use eye shadow under the lower lashes for further enhancement.

ACCESSORIES AND HAIRSTYLING

Sometimes the selection of eye-catching accessories can work wonders in drawing away focus from problems in the eye and forehead areas. For instance, women who have wrinkles on the forehead and around the eyes can accentuate the mouth with bright lipstick, or draw attention to the neck with attractive scarves and necklaces. Hats that cover or cut across the forehead also work well. Men can use interesting ties, sweaters, pocket squares, and shirts to bring the focus downward.

Hairstyles also can be selected to camouflage or detract from problem areas. Among the recommendations:

1. *Eyes too deep-set*. Pull hair toward the face at the forehead and cheekbones and add blonde highlights at the temples to make eyes appear larger and wider.

2. *Low forehead*. Avoid bangs, and use soft fullness at the crown to open up and lengthen the face. Sweep hair off the face and create a more expansive look with a lighter hair color, or add blonde highlights at the front hairline to add length to the face. Men should avoid brushing hair forward; part hair on the side and brush away from the face.

3. *High or broad/wide forehead.* Try deep, full bangs. Place highlighting from the crown to the tips of bangs and on the sides, to play up the eyes and shorten the face.

4. *Bad hairlines.* Bring hair toward the forehead or over the hairline; try partial bangs.

SETTING YOUR SIGHTS ON EYE CARE

As I mentioned earlier, an estimated four-fifths of our knowledge is gained through sight, so it isn't surprising that a Gallup poll[36] reported that Americans fear the loss of vision more than any other medical adversity!

If discovered and treated promptly, many vision problems can be corrected with glasses or contact lenses. Also, studies indicate that almost 90 percent of all eye injuries can be prevented by taking the proper precautionary measures. The most basic steps for eye care are:

1. Have regular eye examinations.
2. Treat the skin around the eyes gently.
3. Observe safety rules when engaging in work, sports, and other activities that may endanger the eyes.
4. Wear eye guards or protective glasses when circumstances dictate.

As with most medical problems, the key to correction of many vision problems is early diagnosis. Vision care experts recommend that from age 20 to age 35, people should have their eyes checked at least once every two years. After 35, it's wise to begin annual examinations, as the chances of cataracts, glaucoma, and deteriorating vision increase. If you wear glasses or contact lenses, be alert to any changes in your vision and have the prescription checked at the first sign of trouble.

A thorough eye examination should usually last from 25 to 60 minutes, depending on the tests you may need. Both a vision and a medical examination should be included, meaning tests for visual ability as well as a check-up of the eyes themselves. Some of the most important areas to be covered in an exam are reactions to light, ability to focus, color vision, eye movements, and condition of the blood vessels, retina, and other parts of the eye. Moreover, you should always have your internal eye pressure checked for signs of glaucoma.

DAY-TO-DAY EYE CARE

Although your vision and eye health may be fine, many ordinary activities and environmental conditions can lead to injury or eyestrain. Here are some day-to-day precautions to help you prevent or alleviate eyestrain:

1. Going without glasses or contacts when you need them, or wearing old prescriptions despite vision changes, can be most damaging to your eyes and your appearance. Straining to see clearly puts undue stress on your eyes and can result in tension lines around the eyes and on the forehead. Make sure eyewear fits properly, is cleaned carefully, and is worn whenever necessary.
2. You may experience eyestrain (aches, burning, or a scratchy feeling in the eyes) because of a drop in blood sugar levels

that often occurs in the late afternoon or after a great deal of close work. To help stabilize blood sugar levels and increase your energy, reduce your daily intake of sweets, caffeine, and nicotine while increasing your intake of water, protein, fresh fruits, and vegetables.

3. Vitamin A is an important factor in good vision. If you have trouble seeing in the dark, suffer from constant eyestrain, or are easily blinded by bright light, you may have a vitamin A deficiency. Check with your doctor. You may also need a carefully structured program of dietary supplements. Don't try self-prescription for vitamin A supplement levels. This vitamin can be toxic if you exceed your daily needs.

4. Infected sinuses can also contribute to burning, swollen eyes. Many sinusitis sufferers find that clearing up the infection greatly relieves eye problems.

5. When watching television, have plenty of light in the room and sit at least six feet away from the screen (further from a color set; it emits more radiation). Look away every 20 minutes or so to relax the eye muscles.

6. For desk work—or any close, concentrated activity such as reading, sewing, or writing—rest your eyes every 20 minutes. Try focusing on something far away, or close your eyes for a few minutes. Whenever possible, use natural light. Let comfort be your guide, choosing illumination that is neither too dim nor too bright. General lighting combined with spot lighting on the work area is best, and avoid shadows. Good posture is also essential—sit upright, relaxed, with your back well supported. It is also wise to tilt your desk or work surface; flat surfaces place you in an abnormal position for viewing.

7. If you must work in fluorescent lighting, take frequent breaks. Leave the room, walk a bit, rest your eyes—whatever you can do in the course of your day to relieve the strain.

8. Recent studies indicate that natural light is essential to our physical, emotional, and visual well-being. The light received through the eyes influences the endocrine system, calcium absorption, sexual development, and resistance to colds and other viral infections. The increasing awareness of the need for "full-spectrum" light—light that contains both the visible spectrum and invisible rays found in natural sunlight—has led to the development of indoor lighting sources that provide full-spectrum lighting. You may want to investigate the advantages of these light sources for your home and work area.

INJURY PREVENTION

Many people are unaware of the damage that sunlamps, tanning centers, and overexposure to sunlight can wreak on the eyes. The most common excuse for not protecting the eyes under these conditions is the desire to avoid white circles around the eyes—but it is far better to disguise these circles with makeup than risk burns. Always wear protective goggles if you must use a sunlamp or tanning booth. Cotton balls or regular sunglasses won't do the job.

When sunbathing, skiing, or working for prolonged periods in bright sunlight, do wear sunglasses (invest in prescription sunglasses if you need to). Gray or smoke-colored lenses are least likely to distort light and colors, with green or brown a good second choice. Avoid blue, pink, orange, or yellow tints. Remove sunglasses indoors, and don't wear them at night; they may eventually impair night vision.

In addition to observing basic sports safety rules and good manners, you should wear eyeguards or appropriate protective glasses when engaging in sports activities. Glasses must be made from impact-resistant glass or plastic, but few are impact-*proof*. Many cannot withstand the force of a smashed tennis ball or racquet, so exercise caution.

While many athletes have turned to contact lenses for sports, these need protection as well. There are industrial and sports-variety eyeguards available, with or without prescription lenses, which are comfortable and valuable for eye safety.

Safety goggles are also a must for yard work. (Stones thrown from a lawn mower or clippings from electric hedge clippers can severely injure the eyes.) Wear them when using chemicals, pesticides, and paint, too.

Finally, heavily chlorinated pools may lead to burned and inflamed eyes, and swimming in pools or lakes may cause eye infections. Wear water-tight swim goggles, keep towels scrupulously clean, and keep your hands away from your eyes to minimize these risks. Prescription diving goggles should be worn by myopic scuba and snorkeling enthusiasts, so you won't strain your eyes while enjoying these activities.

TRENDS IN EYEWEAR

Glasses have become an interesting facet of modern fashion. Today, frames come in so many types, colors, styles, and sizes that

Old-style bifocals   New-style bifocals

you should easily find a frame suitable for your face and lifestyle. Some people have a "wardrobe" of glasses for different occasions. Here again, it's a good idea to comparison shop—prices may vary a great deal, and designer labels tend to be more expensive than many other styles.

For some individuals, eyeglasses are a well-considered aspect of their total image. Auto magnate Lee Iacocca, baseball ace Reggie Jackson, television hosts Phil Donahue and Bill Moyers, film luminaries Woody Allen and Sophia Loren, and feminist writer Gloria Steinem are seldom seen without their eyeglasses.

The newest trend in eyeglasses is the development of a new style of bifocals which do not have a dividing line between the reading and distance portions of the lens. While these glasses are no longer a "give-away" of age, as many people have considered bifocals to be, they are also trickier to fit and manufacture. Be sure to have your prescription checked after having it filled to assure its accuracy and avoid vision problems.

When selecting eyeglass frames, here are some suggestions for choosing styles that will highlight good facial features and play down those that are less attractive.

1. In most cases, a frame that contrasts with your facial shape will add interest and definition. For example:
   • Round face—square or octagonal frames
   • Square/rectangular face—round frames
   • Triangular/heart-shaped face—oval frames

2. The smaller and more delicate the wearer's facial features, the lighter (thinner) the frames should be. The larger and broader the features, the heavier (thicker) the frames. A medium-weight frame is a good choice for those with average features.

3. Men whose facial features aren't strong enough for a heavy frame can still achieve the heavy look by choosing a medium-weight frame in a dark color. This also works well for short men who have large, broad facial features.

4. Women with small, delicate features can achieve a lighter look with a medium-weight frame in today's popular semi-rimless style.

5. To make close-set eyes appear further apart, wear colored frames with a clear bridge over the nose. The frame's color lines should run horizontally.
6. To add lift to a face that's begun to age, try a frame with an upsweep on either the upper or lower rim.

Color is an important fashion consideration in lens and frame selection. You can choose a solid-tinted lens that quietly becomes a part of the frame coloring or opt for a gradient tinting of the same color that goes from the palest shade at the bottom to the deepest at the top of the lens, creating a high-style effect.

A new approach is the tinting of two or three gradient colors that appear and disappear subtly in the lens, allowing the wearer to see through the clearest part. The total effect is a personalized lens that gives depth and drama to eyes and skin tones, while minimizing lines and fatigue shadows.

Optometrists say pale fashion-lens tints usually won't affect color perception and can generally be worn for most day and evening activities. Lens tints of deep intensity, however, can affect color perception somewhat and aren't recommended for full-time wear.

The selection of frame and lens colors is based largely on personal preferences. Skin tones and hair color can, however, serve as general guidelines. The following chart presents some ideas for selection of appropriate colors.

EYEGLASS FRAME CHART

Skin Tone	Suggested Frame Color
Sallow (yellow)	Warm shades of plum or red, amber, reddish-brown, pink, royal blue
Ruddy	Cool shades of blue or green
Pale	Pastel or pale gradients
Gray (due to aging or poor circulation)	Warmer tones of brown or amber, gold
Olive	Reddish-brown, brown, deep blue, red, amber
Pink	Green, yellow, cool brown

These same skin-tone guidelines can be used when selecting tinted lenses to go with today's fashion frames.

Hair Color	Suggested Frame Color
Blonde	Pastels, light tortoiseshell, gold
Light brown	Dark brown, dark red, tortoiseshell, greens and blues that are not bright, gold
Brunette	Dark brown, all bright colors
Black	Black, all bright colors, gold, silver
Red	Greens, bright colors except reds and oranges, gold
Gray	Pale tints of blue or rose, silver
White	Gray, pastel tints, silver

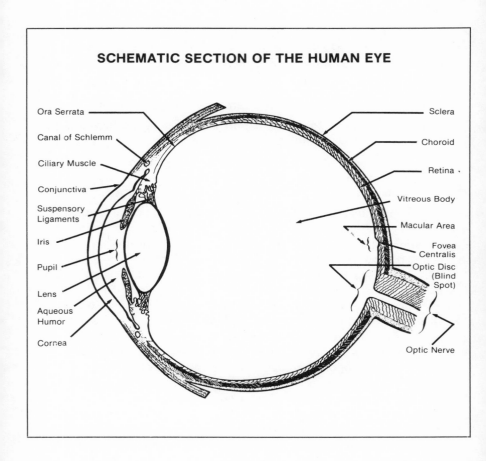

SCHEMATIC SECTION OF THE HUMAN EYE

Ora Serrata

Canal of Schlemm

Ciliary Muscle

Conjunctiva

Suspensory Ligaments

Iris

Pupil

Lens

Aqueous Humor

Cornea

Sclera

Choroid

Retina

Vitreous Body

Macular Area

Fovea Centralis

Optic Disc (Blind Spot)

Optic Nerve

CONTACT LENS SELECTION

Contact lenses are worn by an estimated 14 million Americans—including President Reagan, who has been a contact wearer for forty years.

Appearance is probably the major reason most people select contact lenses. Although eyeglasses can be very attractive, they do hide part of the face. And for those who are extremely nearsighted, glasses with very thick lenses distort the way their eyes look to others. In these cases contacts definitely can improve appearance.

While appearance is the most obvious reason for using contacts, there are other advantages:

139

1. Contacts seem to provide more natural vision, since they fit snugly over the eye and move with the eye, permitting vision through the center where sight is sharpest.

2. Contacts are less easily scratched or broken than glasses.

3. There are no frames to interfere with peripheral vision.

4. Contacts don't fog and are more convenient, since they don't have to be constantly put on or taken off.

5. Researchers are discovering that many contact wearers need not change prescriptions as often as eyeglass wearers. Also, some medical problems are best treated with contacts.

Of course, there are problems that may stem from using contacts. Some people can't adjust to wearing them because of pain or irritation. Others don't adhere to the strict cleaning schedule required before or after each wearing. Others have vision problems or diseases that contact lenses can't correct. However, because contacts offer so many benefits, research continues toward eliminating the drawbacks and limitations. For example, soft lenses were developed to help those who could not tolerate the hard ones. While soft lenses don't last as long, they're more comfortable.

Permanent-wear contact lenses are a relatively new development; however, some ophthalmologists have reservations about their desirability. According to Dr. Daniel Eichenbaum of New York City and Delray Beach, Florida, "They restrict access of nutrients to and are a chronic irritant on the cornea. My preference is for daily-wear contacts because any problems that arise during the day are repaired at night while the lens isn't in the eye. Also, the daily-wear lens is re-sterilized after each wearing, while the permanent lenses are cleaned only when they are removed by the patient's doctor."

The ability to wear contacts comfortably may decrease with age due to reduced lubrication and diminished lid action. Lubrication helps prevent irritation, and lid action is the device that keeps the tears flowing.

EYE SURGERY

Cataracts (a clouding of the lens of the eye that causes partial or total blindness) are obvious to observers because the lens of the eye becomes opaque in appearance. Although commonly associated with aging (cataracts normally occur between ages 55 and 85), they can appear at any age due to an injury, radiation, or the use of certain drugs. There also are hereditary factors which cause the occurrence of cataracts at an early age in some families.

Cataracts can be removed by two different surgical methods. The more conventional method involves pulling out the entire cataract in one piece. This requires the rupture of the ligaments which attach the lens to the eye. Because this procedure can result in complications, Dr. Eichenbaum and many other surgeons use delicate instruments to perform a newer form of surgery—micromechanical surgery.

The delicate instruments allow the surgery to be performed in a closed-eye system—every piece of diseased tissue removed is replaced by clear, saline solution allowing the eye to remain round during surgery. Also, this type of surgery leaves the clear lens capsule (envelope) in the eye, allowing the normal anatomy to be preserved and reducing the chances of complications. "Micromechanical surgery by which we remove cataracts in smaller pieces is gentler for the eye," Dr. Eichenbaum says.

When the cataract is removed, the eye's natural lens power is eliminated. Therefore, patients will need either very strong glasses, contact lenses, or a plastic lens permanently implanted in the eye to correct vision. The latter is the method preferred by Dr. Eichenbaum: "This lens implant procedure has been widely used for more than twenty years and is quite successful. There is no danger to the eye. The plastic material used is known to be well-tolerated by the eye. It can't be rejected (like a kidney transplant) because the implant isn't living tissue."

A newer surgical procedure for the correction of a different type of visual problem is still controversial. Dr. Eichenbaum explains: "Radial keratotomy is a relatively simple procedure in which multiple incisions are made in the cornea, which effectively flattens the cornea and corrects or reduces myopia (nearsightedness). This isn't a procedure which everyone should have, however. Because it's so new, the possible long-term side effects aren't known. If you can wear contact lenses or glasses with reasonable ease, it's advisable to stick with these choices instead of undergoing surgery."

Dr. Eichenbaum describes the type of person who can benefit from radial keratotomy as "someone who has a good reason not to wear glasses or contact lenses. For instance, one of my patients worked in an auto body shop. He was myopic, but the shop was hot and his eyeglasses kept falling off. He couldn't use contacts because of the dirt, paint, and other chemicals around which he worked.

This operation made it possible for him to do his work more effectively and comfortably."

Crossed eyes are another problem that affects appearance. As we all know, talking to a person whose eyes don't both focus on you can be disconcerting. The problem of having one eye out of alignment is called strabismus. It can lead to a condition known as "lazy eye" (amblyopia) in which one eye is significantly stronger than the other. This causes the weaker eye to drift instead of focusing in a line with the stronger eye. If the condition isn't corrected in early childhood, it becomes more difficult to straighten the "lazy eye." However, anyone with amblyopia, even an adult, should seek professional advice.

The loss of an eye due to accident or illness has an impact on appearance as well as on a person's emotional state. Prosthetic eyes are so well-designed that this condition is barely noticeable to most observers, however. Peter Falk, Sammy Davis, Jr., and Sandy Duncan each have a false eye—and Moise Dayan and the "Man in the Hathaway Shirt" brought distinction to the eye patch.

PLASTIC SURGERY
FOR THE EYES AND FOREHEAD

Because the skin on the upper and lower eyelids is the thinnest on your face, it's the first to show the effects of allergy, irritation, unhappiness, sunburn, overindulgence in alcohol, or lack of sleep. As we age, the muscle beneath the eyelid skin begins to thin out and stretch, causing bags and puffiness when fatty-tissue deposits protrude through the weakened muscle. In addition, bags may begin to appear on the eyelids, along with "crow's feet." Sometimes baggy eyelids are hereditary, in which case they may appear in quite young people.

Another common problem in the eye and forehead area is "frown lines"—either vertical or horizontal lines between the eyes or horizontal lines across the forehead.

Fortunately, all of these conditions, which detract from the appearance of both men and women, can be improved through plastic surgery.

1. Blepharoplasty, or eyelid surgery, is taken from the Greek "to mold the eyelids." It is the most frequently performed of all cosmetic surgery procedures—especially for male patients.

   The surgical procedure is simple in concept. Incisions are made on both the upper and lower lids following the lines of

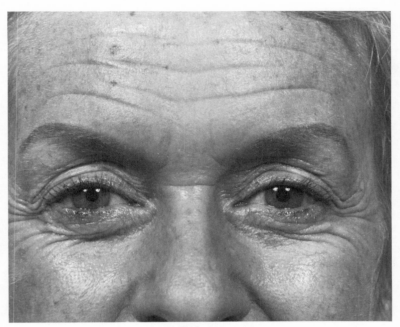

Before

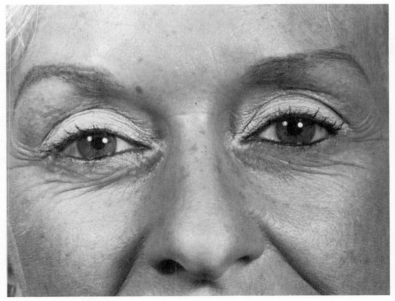

After

the lids. The excess skin and underlying protruding fatty tissue are removed, and the incisions are sutured.

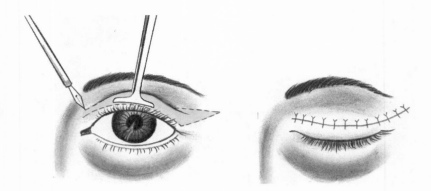

A. Incisions are made along lines that are marked prior to surgery and that result in the suture line on the upper lid being placed in a natural fold of the eye so as to be almost invisible.

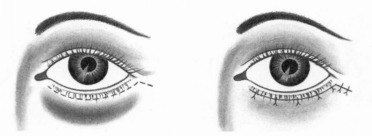

B. The lower lid incision is made beneath the eyelashes, resulting in a very fine and, ultimately, hardly visible line.

A common complication of blepharoplasty is either a lack of tears or excessive tearing immediately following surgery. However, this condition usually abates spontaneously. If the condition persists, it can be treated during an office visit to your surgeon. The other potential complication, superficial "pimples" along suture lines, is also reversible with local treatment.

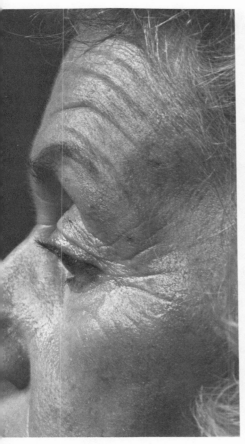
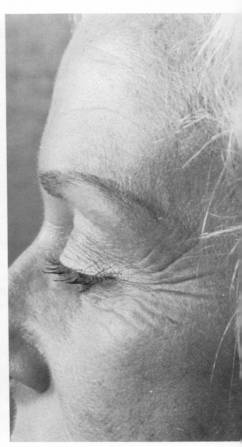

Before   After

Eyelid surgery frequently is performed in conjunction with a full face lift. However, many people—including Joan Kennedy, former First Lady Rosalyn Carter, and hair and beauty expert Vidal Sassoon—prefer to have this procedure long before they have any other noticeable signs of aging.

2. Often an eyebrow lift accompanies surgery to eliminate baggy lids. This procedure is requested when the outer ends of the eyebrows droop so much that they cause the upper eyelids to bulge, pushing them almost on top of the eyelashes. This problem is corrected by making an incision above the droop-

ing brow area or at the hairline and removing a wedge of skin. This results in a more youthful and "wide-eyed" appearance. It also helps reduce "crow's feet." As with blepharoplasty, any scars are hidden.

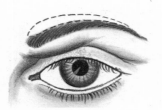 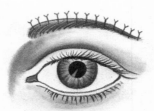

3. Another eyelid problem that sometimes occurs is a congenital deformity called ptosis, an involuntary drooping of one of the upper eyelids due to muscle paralysis. As a result, the eyes appear lopsided. Ptosis can be corrected in a manner similar to blepharoplasty, except that a "spare" tendon is removed from another part of the body and used to replace the paralyzed muscle.

4. Sometimes a person of Oriental heritage asks that his or her eyes be made to conform to the apperance of Occidental eyes. This can be done by creating a fold on the eyelid. An incision is made in the upper lid and a small muscle is attached to the eyelid skin, producing a "Westernized" appearance.

5. Frown lines between the eyes are reduced by making an incision in the eyebrow and removing a section of muscle. No eyebrow hair is removed, and any scarring is almost invisible. Sometimes medical-grade liquid silicone or collagen is injected underneath the skin to help "plump it up."

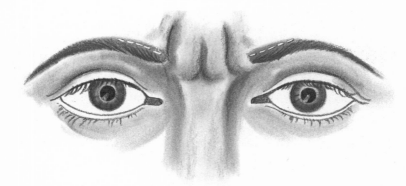

6. A forehead lift, often done in conjunction with a face lift or eyelid surgery, eases horizontal frown lines. An incision is made several inches behind the hairline. Then the underlying muscle is usually removed. Finally, the forehead skin is stretched to the proper position with the excess skin removed. Sometimes the skin is dermabraded (surgically planed, or "sanded," with a high-speed drill). The hair generally hides any scarring; however, if scars are more visible than desired, some revision can be done. As a result of this procedure, the forehead appears higher and eyebrows are elevated a bit more than prior to the surgery.

With the use of an extremely high-powered operating microscope and the delicate instruments used for microsurgery, I've been able to modify the forehead surgery so that the feeling returns much more rapidly than with the standard forehead-lift technique. This occurs because under the intense magnification we can dissect and preserve the forehead nerves of feeling while removing the necessary portions of muscle.

7

CENTERFACE

"There was a young man of devizes,
Whose ears were of different sizes;
    the one that was small
    was no use at all,
But the other won several prizes."[37]

When they're in accord with the rest of the face, our ears and noses generally receive little attention. However, as with the young man in the above limerick, those who have noticeably different or disproportionate ears or noses often are the unfortunate victims of ridicule and rude stereotypes.

Along with our cheeks, these features provide a neutral balance for the, generally, more dramatic-appearing eyes and mouth. We have a number of options for making the most of our "centerface." Among the easiest to learn is the art of contouring: creating illusions through the application of dark and light shading. Models and actors have long used these tricks to present their features in a form other than that dictated by Mother Nature.

The basic principle of contouring is simple: darker shades (contour colors) deemphasize or make areas seem to recede; lighter shades (blushers or highlights) emphasize areas. Contour color won't be as noticeable on darker skins as on light but still can be very effective. Especially for daytime or bright light, go easy on contouring—the goal is a natural appearance, not a muddy or dirty-looking face.

First, the cheekbones. Everyone has them, although many people aren't entirely sure about how to best take advantage of them when applying cheek color. You'll be working in a triangular area bordered by three points: (A) your cheekbone just under the center of your eye; (B) your cheek near the bottom of your ear; and (C) your temple at the top of your ear.

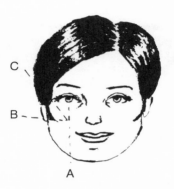

First apply contouring color directly under the cheekbone (you can feel the line with your finger) from the point beneath the center of your eye toward your ear. Blend well so there is no sharp line.

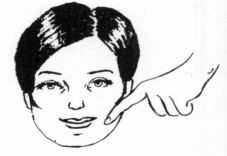

For an oval face, add blusher or highlight color along the cheekbone to the hairline and upward toward the temple. Again, blend well so that no line exists at the jaw, cheekbone, or neck.

For a round face, add blusher in an upward-curving crescent shape on and below the cheekbone, ending before the hairline. You also may start the color a little closer to the nose (about an inch), but don't go below the tip of the nose.

For a square/rectangular face, add blusher on the outer edge of the cheekbone in a semicircular shape. Extend toward the hairline and upward toward the temples.

For a heart-shaped/diamond face, add blusher in an inward-curving, half-moon shape, feathering outward toward the hairline.

For a pear-shaped face, add blusher in an upward-curving crescent shape, beginning further away from the nose and extending toward the hairline but not into the temple.

For a wide face, add blusher in a broad-based triangular shape slanted toward the temple.

For a long face, add blusher in a rectangular shape to the outer edge of the cheekbone and extend toward the hairline and temple. Don't go below the tip of the nose.

Subtle contouring can also be used (by men as well as women) to enhance a less than classic nose. The most common complaints about nose shapes, and the remedies, are:

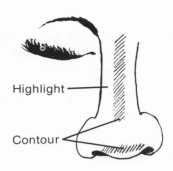

Too thin. Apply a darker shade to the tip and front of the nostrils. Add a lighter shade along the sides of the nose.

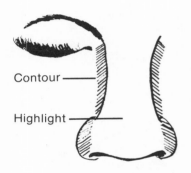

Too wide. Use a lighter shade down the center of the nose; blend a darker shade along the sides.

Too short. Blend lighter shading down the center of the nose from eyebrow level to tip.

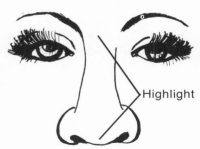

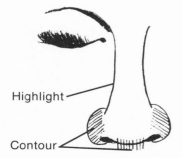

Too long. Smooth a darker shade around the edges of the nostrils and below the tip of the nose. Apply a lighter shade along the sides.

Prominent. Use a lighter shade to highlight the cheek area next to the nose, but don't apply a darker shade to the entire nose (this will draw more attention).

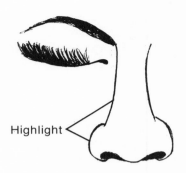

Highlight

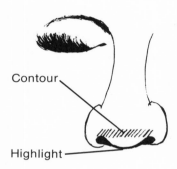

Contour

Highlight

Hooked. Apply a lighter shade underneath the tip of the nose. Add a small amount of darker shade on the tip.

Crooked. Apply a darker shade to areas on the sides that curve outward. Blend a lighter shade in a straight line down the center of the nose.

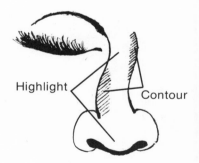

Highlight

Contour

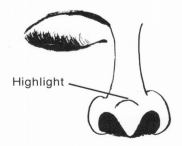

Highlight

Turned up. Blend a lighter shade along the most concave area, but don't extend onto the tip.

Bump. Smooth a little darker shading over the bump. Apply a lighter shade along the sides of the nose.

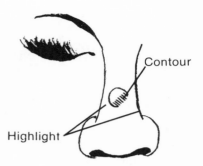

Bridge that curves outward. Apply a darker shade to the curved area. Blend a lighter shade below and above the curve.

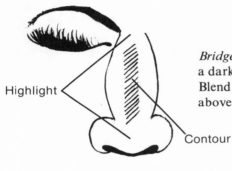

In addition to contouring, women (and men too) can draw attention away from a prominent nose with a hairstyle that adds height and softness on top. A side rather than center part will also help. Men also might want to add a flowing moustache to diminish the appearance of the nose (a small, thin moustache will make a prominent nose seem larger).

155

ENHANCING THE EAR

Ears do more than just transmit auditory signals to our brains as part of the communication process. They're also a readily visible element in the total impression others have of our head and face.

Normal ears are well-shaped, balanced in size in relation to the rest of the head, and don't stick out. If you're among those with this pleasing ear type, they can be an asset to your appearance. However, when ears lack one or more of the foregoing criteria, we seek ways of camouflaging or altering them. Before we discuss techniques for making the most of your ears' appearance, let's look at the most common problems with ear configurations:

Normal size, one ear protruding creates a problem of balance.

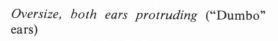

Oversize, both ears protruding ("Dumbo" ears)

Square, both ears protruding (usually has a very small lobe)

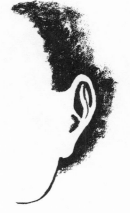

Oversize, flat (a problem with a small head)

Undersize, flat (a problem with a large head)

Normal size, enlarged lobes (a problem frequently occurring as people age and the skin and muscles begin to lose elasticity)

157

Normal size, pointed tops ("Mister Spock" ears, sometimes called "devil-tipped")

Disfigured (this may be from a birth defect or an accident)

Women's choice of earring style is often important in creating a businesslike image and can help deflect attention from ears that vary from the norm. As a general rule for normal ears, simple gold or silver button, ball, or small hoop earrings are best for business wear. Pearls or other understated stones that are in good taste also are acceptable. Cheap, imitation jewelry that lacks distinction detracts from a successful appearance.

To help conceal ear flaws, here are some suggestions: draw attention down and away from protruding or disfigured ears with a hoop or other longer style that extends below the hair covering the ear; camouflage an enlarged lobe or oversize flat ear with a style that covers (but doesn't extend beyond) the lobe, such as a button earring; provide an illusion of length for a small ear with a drop-style earring; and balance a pointed ear top with a triangular earring.

Why do people decide to have their ears pierced? Many women believe that earrings for pierced ears are less likely to be lost; however, if post-type earrings aren't firmly secured, they're almost as susceptible to falling off as nonpierced styles. Although ears can be pierced at home, in a department or jewelry store, or in a

hairstyling salon, this procedure is best done by a nurse or doctor to ensure sterile conditions and guard against infection. If you've had you ears pierced, be sure to follow instructions for the cleaning and care of your ears, especially while they're healing.

Because many women are allergic to certain metals (even gold in some cases), stainless steel is generally considered the best material for the temporary earrings inserted until the pierced hole is completely healed. Thereafter, gold, silver, or platinum is suggested for earring posts or wires.

CHEEK SURGERY

Sometimes people are born without obvious cheekbones, resulting in a flat-looking face. This condition can be corrected by inserting surgical silicone implants through the mouth or through eyelid incisions and building up the flat area. The same technique that is used to create more obvious cheekbones (an improvement entertainer Cher decided upon several years ago, when she also had her chin lifted) also is used to restore contours to an aging face in which the cheeks' underlying fat pads have sagged downward.

RHINOPLASTY

A much more common form of corrective surgery is the "nose job." Since its development in the early twentieth century, rhinoplasty has probably become the best known of all cosmetic surgery procedures. Phyllis Diller had her nose reshaped more than ten years ago, and Dean Martin is among the list of entertainers reported to have undergone this procedure.

Throughout history, the nose has held a special place in a person's body image. Opinions of what constitutes an attractive nose vary depending on changing cultural and ethnic values. While this important sensory organ enables us to appreciate the fragrances around us, its significance surpasses its biological function.

The nose is our most prominent feature (it covers a third of the face). Despite makeup and hairstyles designed to draw attention away from the nose, it's impossible to camouflage or hide, especially in profile. For this reason, an unattractive or deformed nose or one that isn't in harmony with the rest of your face may cause greater dissatisfaction than signs of aging.

Those with unsightly noses have been taunted by painful nicknames or peer rejection. Self-consciousness may cause these men and women to shy away from social and professional situations that would place them in the spotlight. They may appear to be awkward because they attempt to avoid showing their profile or cover their nose with a hand when talking. There have been notable exceptions, however—like Jimmy Durante, who turned his nose into an asset. Some other men and women have distinguished themselves while sporting noses that are "less than Greek"—Barbra Streisand, Richard Nixon, Bob Hope, and Betty Friedan among them.

However, despite these exceptions, it's no wonder that rhinoplasty for many years was the most popular of all cosmetic surgeries. Although still a much-sought-after procedure, rhinoplasty has recently been surpassed by other procedures, partly because of increased emphasis on ethnic pride, including acceptance of distinctive facial characteristics. Still, some people decide that they will be more confident and feel better about themselves with an adjustment to their nasal contours. For instance, prima ballerina Cynthia Gregory chose to have her Greek nose inherited from her father redesigned because she didn't like the way it looked.

A plastic surgeon or otolaryngologist can resculpt the nose so that it balances the rest of the face. Reducing a large nose, building up scooped-out contours, tilting, straightening, or shortening—all can be achieved with relative ease.

The most difficult part of rhinoplastic surgery is dealing with the patient's expectations. As surgeons we can only work with what you have. For instance, we can't transform a thick-skinned "bulb" into a sculptured aquiline form or create a delicate, tipped nose from thick

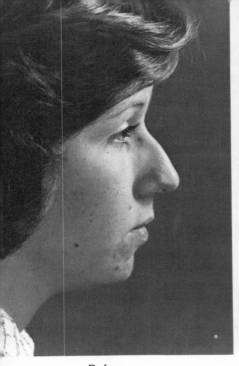
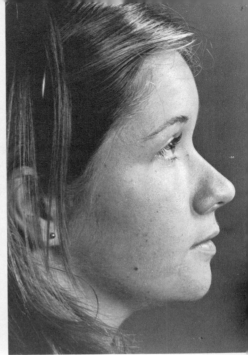

Before   After

skin. Among the factors that influence the configuration which can
be designed are skin thickness and condition, facial shape, bone and
cartilage thickness and shape, hereditary factors, and the patient's
age. Sometimes a chin implant should be done at the same time as
the nose operation for a truly balanced result.

In most cases, the procedure for rhinoplasty does not require any
external incision, so there aren't any scars. For a nose reduction, we
first reduce and refine the bony upper portion of the nose by
breaking and resetting the bones. Then the middle portion is made
of bone and cartilage which must be sculpted. Finally, the nose tip is
refined or is re-formed by working with the four pieces of cartilage
that comprise it.

For nose augmentation (a less common procedure), a pocket is
created along the bridge inside the nasal passage. Then an implant
of surgical silicone or cartilage removed from elsewhere on the
patient's body is carefully carved and inserted into the pocket to
build up the bridge of the nose.

Among the complications sometimes encountered with all nose
procedures are nosebleed, infection, and numbness, all of which are

usually temporary. In addition, the implants for nose augmentation sometimes slip out of position, requiring further corrective surgery.

"Rum Nose"

Rosacea is a skin disorder that plagues many men and women, especially those who are middle-aged. Anyone who has seen a W. C. Fields movie will be familiar with the symptoms: a bulbous, red, and pimply nose with dilated blood vessels.

Although excessive alcohol consumption can be a contributing factor (hence the common name "rum nose"), it is not the only cause of this problem. Unfortunately, moderate and non-drinkers are often stigmatized by rosacea's association with alcoholic intake. Other factors include hot, highly seasoned foods and beverages, especially those containing caffeine, which are vasodilators (blood dilators); high body acidity; and overexposure to extreme climatic conditions.

In milder cases, this condition may be controlled by frequent application of ice or witch hazel to contract the dilated blood vessels. Topical sulfur lotions also may be helpful. Surgical treatment may be necessary for more severe cases.

Ear Repositioning

Another condition that can bring ridicule to its possessor is unusual or protruding ears. "Dumbo" and "elephant ears" are two of the unkind appellations that too often greet those with protruding or unusually shaped ears. Fortunately, these conditions can be corrected through otoplasty, cosmetic surgery for "pinning the ears back." Although most often performed on children, this procedure can also be successfully performed on adults by a plastic surgeon or otolaryngologist.

Otoplasty corrects the condition that causes the ears to protrude from the head rather than conform to the shape of it. In most cases, the cause of this type of deformity is the absence of a fold in the ear, which keeps the ear close to the side of the head. Clark Gable, Warren Beatty, and Bing Crosby all had to deal with protruding ears. Gable apparently was very sensitive about this problem; however prevailing taboos against cosmetic surgery evidently kept him from having his ears corrected.

Otoplasty for this condition is a relatively simple procedure, during which we create the missing fold in the ear using the skin and cartilage already present. During surgery a strip of skin is removed from behind the ear. Then we make an incision in the cartilage and reposition it to form the "fold" that will flatten back the ear. The incision is then sutured. Because the incision and resulting scar are in the folds behind the ear, the scar is barely visible to the naked eye when healed. Infection, which is rare, is the most serious complication with this procedure.

Other ear deformities that can be corrected or improved through cosmetic surgery include reducing ear size, improving the shape and contour of "cauliflower ears" (commonly seen on boxers), and replacing missing earlobes.

HEARING AIDS

Although we can't actually *see* the hearing loss that afflicts 1 out of every 13 Americans, the means of correcting the problem is often quite visible. Microelectronics has made possible tiny transistors, resistors, and microphones that have enabled manufacturers to considerably reduce the size of hearing aids. Still, these corrective devices often are shunned because many men and women with a hearing loss believe a hearing aid will detract from their appearance or because they don't want others to know about their handicap.

Yet, the ability to hear well is essential to the full development of individual capabilities and the enjoyment of life. According to the National Hearing Aid Society, denial of a hearing loss may create personal unhappiness, place an unnecessary burden on family and friends, and cause serious employment problems. Almost half of

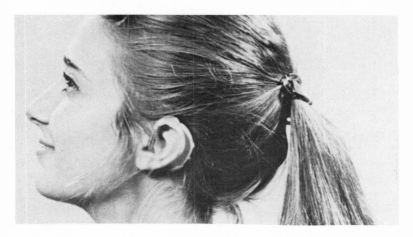

hearing-impaired persons are in the working adult population, the Society's latest figures reveal.

Among other consequences of uncorrected hearing loss, according to the National Hearing Aid Society, are psychological maladjustment, learning disability, deterioration of the quality of speech, withdrawal from society, and a loss of income (estimated at $1.75 billion annually).

A government study[38] showed that the proper fitting of a hearing aid may produce tangible results for the hearing-impaired. When 1,200 hard-of-hearing persons were checked after a year of hearing-aid use, their combined income had risen 790 percent. Certainly one of the best-known hearing-aid wearers—President Ronald Reagan —doesn't seem to have experienced any professional stigma by using this corrective device.

Dr. Marlene Bevan, Director of the Northwestern Michigan Hearing and Speech Center and President of the Academy of Dispensing Audiologists, has conducted one of the few research projects on the effects of wearing a hearing aid on adults. Among her findings (not yet published) were:

1. People suffering hearing loss associate it with aging, although people wearing hearing aids were not perceived to look significantly older than nonwearers.
2. Those who wore hearing aids in both ears were perceived to have greater hearing impairment than those with only one device.
3. There was suspicion that hearing-aid wearers may be less self-assured than nonwearers.
4. The credibility of hearing-aid wearers was not perceived in a detrimental way.
5. Hearing-aid wearers may be considered less attractive as new friends or associates than nonwearers.
6. Reactions in all areas by those who had had some previous experience with someone who was hearing-impaired or wore a hearing aid was less extreme than those of people with no background in this area.

These findings indicate the need for increased public education regarding hearing loss and the use of hearing aids, says Dr. Bevan. "The real fear for people who know nothing about hearing aids or hearing impairment seems to be that communication will not be successful. People are very concerned about their ability to communicate with anyone they think won't be able to understand them.

When you hear:

2. The vibrations of the eardrum cause the bones in the middle ear to move back and forth like tiny levers. This lever action converts the large motions of the eardrum into the shorter, more forceful motions of the stapes.

1. Sound waves enter your ear, travel through the auditory canal, and set up vibrations in the eardrum.

6. In the brain the impulse is translated into the sensation you know as **sound.**

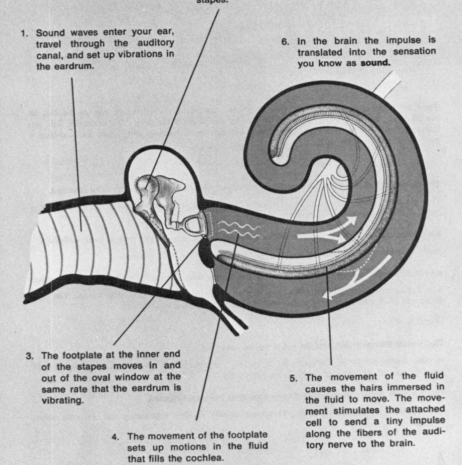

3. The footplate at the inner end of the stapes moves in and out of the oval window at the same rate that the eardrum is vibrating.

5. The movement of the fluid causes the hairs immersed in the fluid to move. The movement stimulates the attached cell to send a tiny impulse along the fibers of the auditory nerve to the brain.

4. The movement of the footplate sets up motions in the fluid that fills the cochlea.

165

Therefore, if hearing aids improve your ability to communicate well, they can be part of a vital image of success."

Hearing loss is due to these major factors: nerve damage to the inner ear caused by birth defects, disease, or aging; accumulated earwax in the external canal; infection of the middle ear; a perforated eardrum; or emotional problems.

Some indications of a possible hearing loss are:

1. Frequent requests to have spoken material repeated.
2. Inconsistent responses to sound.
3. Inattentiveness.
4. Faulty speech.
5. Frequent requests that sounds be made louder, but then an indication that the sound is too loud.
6. Ear infections, constant ringing in the ears, or dizziness.
7. Excessive frustration and withdrawal.

If you suspect that you have experienced a hearing loss, consult a physician. Otologists and otolaryngologists are doctors specializing in the diagnosis and treatment of hearing problems. If no medical or surgical intervention is advised, you may be referred to a hearing-aid specialist (audiologist) or hearing-aid dealer to be tested and fitted for an aid.

The most popular types of hearing aids are:

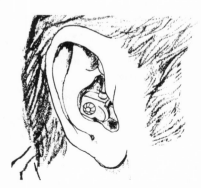

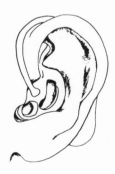

1. *In-the-ear,* which fit directly into the ear and have no external wires.

2. *Behind-the-ear,* which fit snugly behind the ear and are connected to a specially fitted ear mold by a short plastic tube.

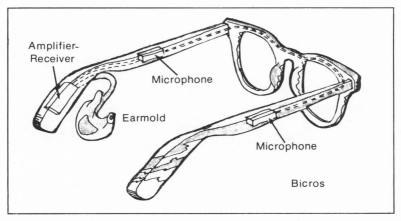

Amplifier-Receiver

Microphone

Earmold

Microphone

Bicros

3. *Eyeglass,* which are built into an eyeglass frame and connected to a tube or specially fitted ear mold that is inserted into the outer ear canal.

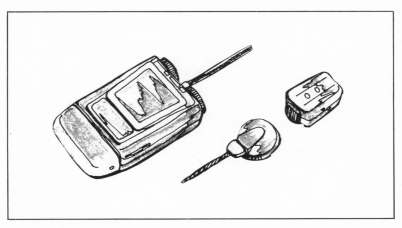

4. *On-the-body,* which has a larger microphone, amplifier, and power supply in a case that can be carried in a pocket and attached by a cord to the receiver, which is connected directly to the ear mold.

In-the-ear hearing aids generally are useful only for mild hearing loss and aren't effective for deafness caused by nerve loss. And, Dr. Bevan's studies indicate that in-the-ear models are no less visible than behind-the-ear and eyeglass styles, unless they're covered by the person's hair.

8

A FIRM BASE

"Thy teeth are like a flock of
sheep that are even shorn,
    which came up from the washing;
Whereof everyone there twins,
    and none is barren among them.
Thy lips are like a thread of scarlett,
    and thy speech is comely; . . .
Thy neck is like the tower of David
builded for an armoury."[39]

Your mouth is more than a vehicle for verbalizing your thoughts, ideas, questions and instructions. It also offers those who meet you a memorable impression of your personality. Your expressions, the shape of your mouth, the condition of your teeth, and, for men, the presence of a moustache and/or beard all contribute to the image others receive about you.

Your chin and neck complete the picture, providing either a firm or a weak base for your face.

COSMETICS

For women, cosmetics present one of the easiest ways to accentuate the positive and deemphasize the negative apsects of this area. The cosmetic arts can bring into better balance nature's imperfections by creating an illusion of harmony.

Naturally, since the mouth is a major focal point, you'll want a range of lip colors to coordinate with your wardrobe and to adapt to the changing seasons. Other staples are a lip-lining pencil (a neutral brown shade blends well with most lip colors) and lip gloss for shiny highlights and moisture. If you have "rivers" (tiny lines surrounding the lips), gloss should be avoided because it tends to run. The following shaping tips are recommended for applying lip color most effectively:

1. If your lips need shaping, apply foundation makeup first to blur the natural edges.
2. Outline the lips in pencil—top lip from inner line of bow, out; bottom lip from corner to corner. The points of the bow should fall directly under the center of each nostril. For lasting color, fill in a first layer of color with lip pencil before adding lipstick.

GUIDE TO LIPCOLORS COORDINATED WITH HAIR COLOR*

Hair Color	Lipcolors
Blonde, white, silver, and gray	Soft pink, lilac, pale orange, soft wine red, clear red, soft earthtones
Light auburn and golden red	Apricot, soft orange, soft rust, golden peach, soft pink, coral, clear red
Dark auburn or copper	All the above colors; may be slightly deeper than for lighter hair
Light to dark brown	Beige tones, clear red, coral, true pink, rose-red, wine-red, plum, soft orange, strawberry red
Dark brown to black	All of the above colors; may be slightly deeper than for lighter hair

*The above charts by permission of the Milady Publishing Corporation, from the Standard Textbook for Professional Estheticians.

3. Using a lip brush, fill in with color (see chart on page 170 for suggested colors). If you use lipstick instead, you may want to try dotting on color, then blending with a brush. Top with gloss for further accent, if you wish, unless your lips are too full or have rivers. For Black women, lipstick that turns purplish may be the result of excess acidity in the skin. Use of a yellow lip-toner beneath the lip color will correct this problem.

Some additional shaping hints are:

1. *For wide lips:* Stop outlining just short of the edges. Use a darker shade in the center, a lighter one toward the edges.

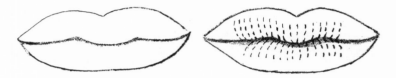

2. *For thin lips:* Use lip-liner on the outer rim of the lips, extending the line slightly at the top, corners, and bottom. Fill in with a lighter shade and gloss.

3. *For full lips:* Line the lips inside the natural lip line. Fill in with a medium shade. You may want to skip the gloss—it will further call attention to the fullness.

4. *For uneven lips:* If the proportions of upper and lower lip are uneven, choose the lip size you prefer for one lip. Then line the other lip to balance, and fill in with color.

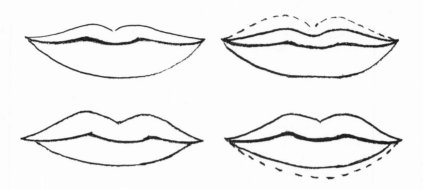

If the shape is off-balance, line the uneven corners and fill in with color.

5. *For cupid's bow:* Widen the lips by applying liner from the highest point on each side of the upper lip and from the deepest part of the lower lip to the outer edges of the mouth. Fill in with color.

6. *For drooping lips:* Line only the corners of the lower lip, adding a lift at the outer edges. On the upper lip, line only the bow. Then apply lip color and blend.

For the chin area, learn to sculpt through contouring, using dark foundation to distract, light foundation to attract the eye.

1. *For a receding chin:* Over foundation, draw a thin line with a lighter shade of makeup from the chin toward the ears; then blend. Add a lot of rouge on the tip of the chin.

Rouge   Highlight

Contour

2. *For a prominent chin:* Over foundation, draw parallel angled lines with a darker shade of makeup just below the ears to the center of the chin; then blend.

173

3. *For a double chin:* Apply a darker foundation along the under edge of the jawbone from the center of the chin to the ears; then blend.

Contour

HAIR/BEARDS/MOUSTACHES

Hairstyles also can help make a problem chin appear in better balance with the rest of the face. Clairol's hair care experts recommend the following for women:

1. *For a strong chin:* Keep hair shorter, and use vertical lines (like soft curls or fullness at the crown) and horizontal lines (like slight fullness at the sides). Concentrate attention on the top. A style that falls directly at the jaw will only add more width; pulling hair straight back will also expose the flaw.

2. *For a narrow chin:* Keep hair longer, and use horizontal lines like curls or fullness at the chin.

3. *For a short neck:* To achieve an appearance of length, lift the style and expose your neck; add height to the crown. Long or shoulder-length hair will make your head sink further into your shoulders.

Just as makeup assists women in accenting assets and hiding flaws, so can neatly trimmed beards and/or moustaches help define a man's face and add interest to his appearance.

Peter Hantz says that the shapes of beards and moustaches are like common sense. If you have a long, thin face and want to make it look longer and thinner, you wear a goatee. If you want to make it look more in proportion, you wear a moustache and thick sideburns. A full beard also will fill out a thin face.

If you have a heavy face, cut your sideburns on an angle going toward the mouth. Then add a narrow moustache in the '40s style. A square jaw can be minimized with a soft, rounded beard.

Men with weak chins should go with a full beard and moustache, since a moustache alone will emphasize a lack of chin line.

Beards or moustaches often are grown by younger men who want to appear more mature—a decision with which Mr. Hantz agrees.

Some men, however, shouldn't wear beards at all. "A man like Robert Redford who has large pores in his skin will find that a beard makes him look even more pockmarked," he warns.

Fair-haired men who want to wear a moustache will get a better effect if they touch it up with a little light-brown hair color. A man whose beard or moustache is graying might want to do the same —or leave it natural for an attractive salt-and-pepper effect.

Caring for a beard and/or moustache is relatively easy. Shampoo every day, since facial hair traps perspiration, and use conditioner to keep the hair soft. Combing, brushing, and regular trimming also are important for a well-groomed appearance.

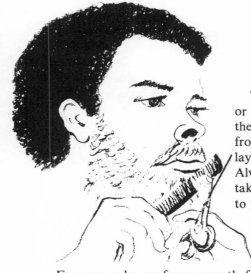

The easiest way to trim a beard or moustache is to comb through the hair in the opposite direction from which it grows, then cut each layer so that all layers are even. Always use sharp scissors, and take care to avoid cutting too close to your nose and ears.

For men who prefer a smooth face, shaving can be a distinct nuisance, especially when complicated by ingrown hairs. Personal preference determines the shaving method. Some men swear by their razor and blade; others will use nothing but an electric shaver. Here are some tips, whatever your preference:

1. *Electric shaver.* Your face should be as dry as possible to begin. Application of a pre-shave will rid the skin of oils that make the shaver slide over hairs and will make hairs stand on end to be more easily accessible to the blades. Aftershave may soothe irritation, but the alcohol content causes drying, so use a moisturizer instead to protect your skin.

2. *Razor and blade.* This method needs the opposite atmosphere: the wetter the better. Use a washcloth soaked in very warm water to soften your beard for shaving. Once your face is good and wet, apply a shaving cream with an effective lubricating ingredient. Use a sharp blade and careful strokes. Take your time; haste makes nicks and cuts.

3. *Ingrown beard hairs.* These result from shaving with a dull blade, shaving too close, or naturally curly hair (curled beard hairs may curve back into the skin). If you have more than an occasional occurrence, try using a sharp blade every time, shave less often, and don't shave against the grain. You might even try letting your beard grow, at least long enough to clear up the irritation and allow the hairs to grow out completely.

Sometimes facial hair is definitely unwelcome—especially for women. According to the International Guild of Professional Electrologists, as many as 90 percent of women experience some problems with superfluous hair. The basic causes are heredity, normal hormonal changes that occur as a woman ages, and the use of certain drugs (such as birth control pills and some postpartum medications).

There are several choices for dealing with unwanted hair on the upper lip, chin, and cheeks. Many women find regular bleaching a satisfactory solution; others, however, prefer either temporary or permanent removal of the hair.

Temporary methods include tweezing (if there are only a few offending hairs) and cream or wax depilatories. Cream depilatories remove unwanted hair by chemically softening and dissolving the hair shaft; however, they don't destroy the root. When using a cream depilatory on the face, be sure the label states that it's designed for that purpose—and do a patch test first, since many people are allergic to these items.

Waxing removes hair from the roots and is best done by a trained professional—at least for the first few times, so you can learn the proper technique. In this process, hot wax is applied to the area from which hair is to be removed and allowed to harden. Then it's pulled off with a quick jerk. My opinion is that facial waxing continued on a regular basis can have an adverse effect on the delicate skin of the face, contributing to the wrinkling process.

Facial hair can be permanently removed by electrolysis, a procedure increasingly sought by both men and women. This should only be performed by a well-trained professional. Anna Crispen, an expert electrologist frequently recommended by dermatologists in New York City, says women primarily have electrolysis to remove hair on the upper lip, chin, and cheeks, while men are concerned about hair on their cheeks and sideburn area or about ingrown hairs (as mentioned previously). Other areas frequently treated with electrolysis are the top and bridge of the nose and the edge of the ears.

The electrolysis technique is described in Chapter 4. During an initial consultation, find out the costs and be wary of unrealistic guarantees and the citing of unreasonably short time periods. Too much, too soon could lead to painful results.

Most electrolysis procedures will require several visits, depending on the amount of hair to be removed. Ms. Crispen estimates the number of hours necessary for the following procedures: upper lip—two to six; chin—one to six; cheeks—two; sideburns—two to five; top of nose—one to two; bridge of nose—one; edge of ears—one to three.

A word of caution for those with spider veins (areas of broken capillaries near the skin surface): waxing may cause special problems for you. Pulling and stretching the skin can cause bleeding or, at the very least, great discomfort. Check with your doctor first. A cream depilatory might be the safest method to avoid bruising of skin and veins.

BASIC TEETH CARE

There's one type of face lift that takes only seconds to perform: *a smile.* A few pennies and minutes a day can help you keep your million-dollar smile for life—and will do wonders for your outlook and appearance.

Unfortunately, because of dental problems, some people are afraid to smile, while others cover their mouth with a hand when talking.

Dr. Cherilyn G. Sheets, a dentist in Inglewood and Newport Beach, California, says many people feel ill-at-ease and unable to compete successfully in the work world because they believe their teeth are unattractive. "With the mouth we express everything from laughter to love. When people think their teeth detract from the appearance of their mouth, they often feel unhappy about the rest of their appearance as well. Something as simple as older fillings that are turning dark can sometimes make a person self-conscious."

Fortunately, modern dental tehcniques and equipment make correction of most problems a relatively easy process. And the results can lead to a better image. For example, Dr. Sheets says, "One of my patients was a professional woman who had little pits in her teeth—like dark dots—because the enamel hadn't formed properly. The teeth weren't decayed, but she felt the pitting made her look slothful, as though she didn't take care of herself. After we capped the pitted teeth, she became more confident and even went back to

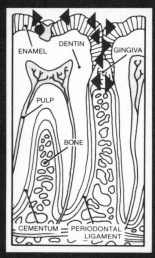

1. ENAMEL, the hard, outer protective covering of the tooth is attacked by the acid. This is the beginning of the decay process.

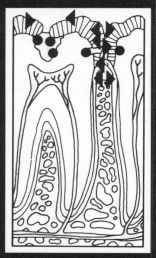

2. The decay spreads into the DENTIN, a softer layer that forms the bulk of the tooth.

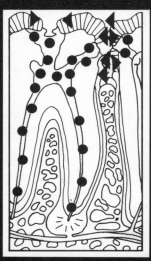

3. If the infection spreads to the PULP, the soft center tissue containing blood vessels and nerve tissue, an abscess can form at the root of the tooth.

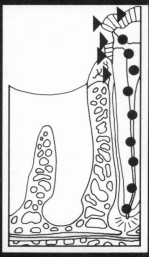

4. If not treated by endodontic (root canal) therapy, the tooth may be lost.

school to get a masters' degree so she could vie for a higher-paying position. She felt her changed appearance would allow her to compete on a stronger basis."

There are two key factors in the prevention of dental problems: plaque control and fluoride treatments.

1. *Dental plaque* is the sticky, invisible film of bacteria that forms constantly on your teeth. When you eat, the bacteria in plaque use the sugars in your food as an energy source. As part of this procedure, acids are produced that attack the enamel surface of your teeth. The extent of damage depends on how hard the tooth enamel is, how strong the acids are, and how long they remain on your teeth (the most damage occurs within the first 20 minutes after eating sugars). Once the acids have broken through the enamel, decay results.

Brushing correctly and frequently and flossing daily are the major steps in plaque control. Here are a few simple pointers for proper teeth care:

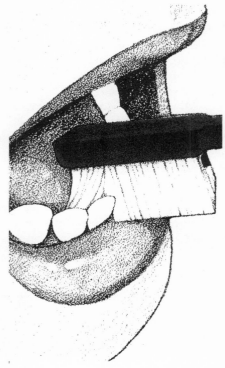

- Invest in the right tools. A soft-bristled brush, dental floss, and disclosing agents (tablets or solutions which, when used, show areas where plaque is building up and spots missed in brushing) are what you'll need to maintain teeth and gums between regular check-ups.

- Brush vertically and then from side to side in short, gentle scrubbing motions using a flouride toothpaste. Holding your brush at a 45° angle to the gums and brushing from side to side in a gentle scrubbing motion is an effective method for cleaning teeth and removeing plaque.

- Use the disclosing agents to see where plaque is forming so you may brush and floss more effectively.

- To floss:
  a. Wrap a length of floss around both middle fingers, using the index fingers and thumbs to control the direction of the flossing.

  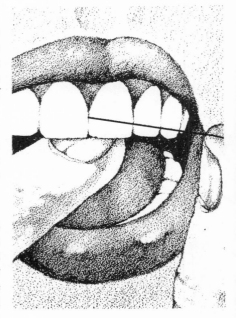

  b. Holding the floss tightly, insert it between the teeth, using a "sawing" motion.

  c. When the floss reaches the gumline, curve it into a "C" shape against one tooth and gently slide it into the space between the gum and the tooth until you feel resistance. Be careful not to press too hard on the gums. Move the floss away from the gum, scraping the side of the tooth. Particles of food and plaque adhere to the floss and come out with it.

  d. Next, curve the floss around the other tooth and scrape it, too.

  e. Repeat with all teeth, once a day. Don't forget back teeth!

- Brush your tongue gently when brushing teeth. Particles of food and bacteria can be found there as well.

2. *Flouride* is essential for strengthening tooth enamel and the supporting bone structure. In addition to drinking fluoridated water (the best source of this nutrient) and using fluoride toothpastes, you can protect your teeth with topical fluoride treatments (a gel, liquid, or paste applied by the dentist) or with daily use of fluoride mouth rinse, which is available without prescription in most drugstores.

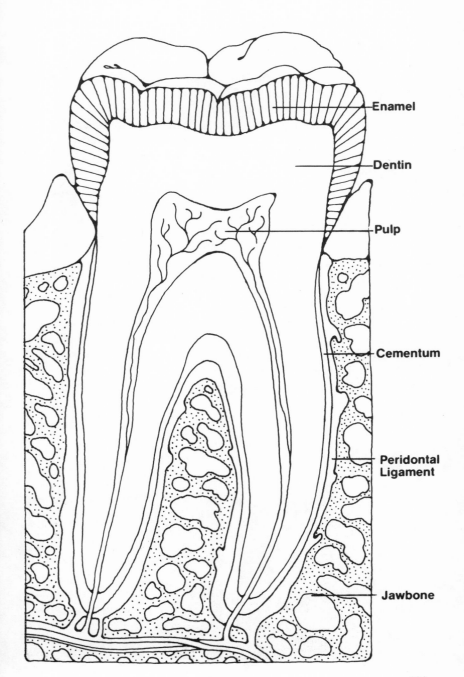

Enamel

Dentin

Pulp

Cementum

Peridontal
Ligament

Jawbone

183

DENTAL TREATMENT

Stains, decay, gaps between teeth, and chipped or irregular teeth are among the most common dental conditions that affect appearance. Thanks to modern dental techniques and materials, all these situations can easily be remedied.

Stains may result from a variety of causes. Among the most frequent local offenders are nicotine, caffeine, and tea, which cause surface stains. The use of certain drugs (particularly tetracyclines) can also cause permanent discolorations, which can go all the way through the tooth. In addition, staining can result from the death of a tooth pulp. There are two ways of having stains removed:

1. *Bleaching.* Many stains can be eliminated with a bleaching process, which is a painless and inexpensive procedure. The most frequent drawback with bleaching is that the color may not be an exact match with that of surrounding teeth.
2. *Capping, Bonding, and Filling.* Tetracycline stains, along with many other tooth appearance problems, can be remedied through either capping (crowning) or bonding techniques.

Capping involves grinding down the tooth or teeth involved and protecting them with a porcelain or porcelain-fused-to-gold cap that's tinted to match the other teeth. Capping often can save a tooth which otherwise might have been pulled because of decay or breakage. Also, according to Dr. Sheets, capping sometimes can correct a malocclusion (bite) problem.

Before capping

After capping

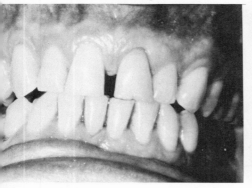
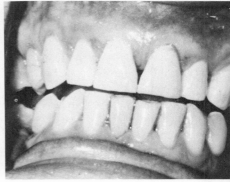

Bonding is a newer procedure, where the stained or misshapen tooth is etched with a very mild acid (similar to the acid found in lemon juice) that forms miscroscopic irregularities in the tooth's enamel surface. Next a liquid plastic is painted onto the tooth surface and then hardened through a chemical or light-curing process. The bonded resin covers imperfections and discolored spots and fills in chipped areas. This also can work for very badly misshapen front teeth, or to fill gaps between teeth. A similar method is to bond thin acrylic shells or laminated veneers directly to the front surface of the tooth with the liquid plastic material.

Bonding has certain advantages over capping: the tooth structure isn't destroyed or basically altered; the procedure can be done in one appointment; and it's relatively painless. It's also about one-third to one-half the cost of capping.

However, capping offers long-term durability, whereas bonding may last an average of only five years before the procedure must be repeated. Also, the resin material may wear off or become stained (a problem not encountered with capping).

Fillings remain the standard procedure for dealing with the majority of decayed or chipped teeth. Silver and gold are the strongest materials for this procedure and generally are recommended for filling teeth at the back of the mouth because of chewing stress. Composite resins are most often used on front teeth, where appearance is important. However, these compounds can stain and usually won't last as long as metal fillings.

PERIODONTAL TREATMENT

Even if you've never had a cavity, you could lose your teeth due to the major cause of tooth loss in adults—periodontal (gum) disease, which most adults will encounter at some point in their lives, according to the American Academy of Periodontology.

This progressively dangerous disease affects the tissues and membranes that support the teeth in the jawbone and usually begins as an inflammation of the gums. If neglected, the gums become more inflamed, bleed, swell, and lose their ability to support the teeth. Eventually, the teeth will loosen and fall out.

Unlike some diseases, periodontal problems are preventable by proper and frequent tooth brushing, flossing and professional cleaning.

Among the factors that contribute to gum disease are plaque

buildup and certain medical conditions (such as pregnancy, diabetes, thyroid disease and blood conditions) and medications. The beginning signs of periodontal disease include:

- Gums that bleed easily
- Puffy, red, or tender gums
- Pus between the teeth and gums
- Loose teeth
- Receding gums
- Persistent bad breath and/or bad taste in mouth

Any of these symptoms is a message to see your dentist immediately. If you have periodontal disease, a dentist or periodontist will have to remove the plaque and calculus (hardened plaque) from your teeth. In its more serious forms, periodontal disease may require some type of surgical procedure to re-contour the tooth-supporting bone and gums.

ORTHODONTICS

There was a time when most people believed that orthodontic devices were only for children. Today, increasing numbers of adults —including former "Miss America" Shirley Cothram Barrett—can be observed wearing braces, the most visible form of orthodontic treatment. According to the American Association of Orthodontists, one of every six orthodontic patients is an adult seeking correction for such problems as spaces between the teeth, protruding front teeth ("buck teeth"), and crooked or crowded teeth.

Often these problems can be solved by the use of braces. Braces may take several forms, depending on the type of orthodontic problems and the patient's desires. Most often, these are metal appliances that are attached to the teeth for the duration of the treatment period. Braces have changed considerably during the past twenty-five years, says Dr. Lee Graber, an orthodontist in Kenilworth, Illinois, and Associate Professor of Orthodontics at Chicago's Loyola University. "They're less conspicuous, smaller, and work with thinner, more comfortable wires. Some modern braces are almost invisible. In addition, we sometimes can use a removable appliance, so patients can go about their regular work life and wear the braces only at home." Ninety to ninety-five percent of these

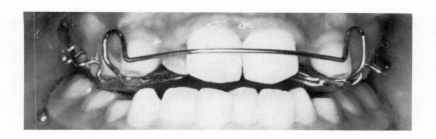

patients have experienced a positive effect on the way they feel about themselves and also on the way other people interact with them. He has observed that many women with orthodontic problems become more adept at using makeup following treatment. "They have something better to work with because the face is more balanced, but they also seem more attuned to how they can use cosmetic aids to their benefit."

Professional football player Harvey Martin of the Dallas Cowboys was one of the estimated 10 million Americans who have a deformed jaw. The problem of his lower jaw jutting out became noticeable in junior high school and got progressively worse. He was teased by other children and became so self-conscious that he refused to let people see him smile. Although his athletic skill brought him professional recognition, he continued to be concerned about his appearance. He also experienced problems in biting and chewing his food. Finally, Martin consulted an orthodontist, who recommended an operation to correct the problem so he could eat comfortably. Following the surgery, Martin says he feels better about himself and is more outgoing. He's also more in demand for television commercial appearances, a lucrative sideline for many professional athletes.

Comedienne Carol Burnett and former First Lady Eleanor Roosevelt are among the best-known examples of the reverse problem—extreme forward positioning of the upper teeth, commonly called "buck teeth." As both a child and an adult, Mrs. Roosevelt suffered from unkind comments about her facial appearance. Later in her life, an accident resulted in oral surgery that helped lessen the problem.

REPLACING MISSING TEETH

Dentists warn that any teeth lost due to illness or accident should be replaced. When missing teeth aren't replaced, the adjacent teeth usually tip into the empty space, and uneven pressure during chewing can result in bone and gum problems.

Either a removable or permanent partial denture can be used to replace several missing teeth.

Replacing a lost tooth with a false one may involve bridgework, where the teeth on either side of the missing tooth are capped and used to anchor the false tooth through a connection at the base of all three. Another possibility is to implant a base beneath the gums and attach a false tooth to that.

If a tooth is knocked out, new "reimplantation" surgery may enable an oral surgeon to reattach your own tooth. Tooth reimplantation has the greatest chance of success when the patient is treated within 30 minutes of the tooth loss. As with reimplanting limbs, a procedure I'm called upon to perform with some frequency, you should get to a hospital emergency room quickly. Do *not* clean the tooth. Wrap it in a wet cloth and take it to your dentist.

When only a few healthy teeth remain, patients now can be fitted with overdentures—instead of having the remaining teeth pulled and being fitted for full dentures as in the past. The procedure for overdentures involves filing down the healthy teeth, which serve as a foundation to which the overdenture is cemented. Oral surgeons say overdentures tend to fit better than full dentures and enable wearers to bite and chew with greater ease.

PLASTIC SURGERY

For some deformities and other problems of the mouth, chin, and neck area, plastic surgery may be the only way to achieve a better appearance. In addition to the chin and mouth surgery already discussed, some of the most common problems with which we deal are building up a receding chin; tightening up jowls and double chins; reducing "rivers," the fine lines around the mouth; and removal of "turkey gobbler" folds on the neck. We also can greatly improve the appearance of those unfortunate people born with a cleft lip or palate.

A receding chin is brought into better proportion with the rest of the face by the simple insertion of a plastic chin implant. The size and shape of the implant (which is carved by the surgeon) are determined by the patient's individual needs, plus surgical considerations. To insert the implant, an incision is made underneath the chin or inside the mouth and a pocket is carved out to hold the implant. Scarring is minimal when the incision is under the chin and

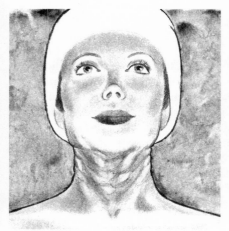

Pre-op neck rejuvenation

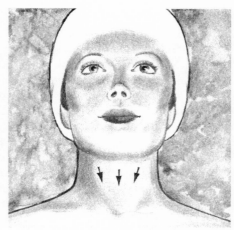

Post-op neck rejuvenation

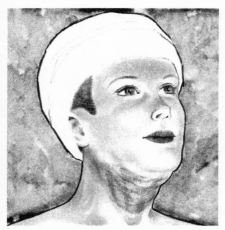

Pre-op neck rejuvenation

Post-op neck rejuvenation

invisible inside the mouth. Sometimes an under-the-chin scar over-develops, but steroid injections will improve this condition. Another possible complication is shifting of the implant, in which case another operation will be performed to correct the situation.

Chinplasty to reduce a double chin frequently is combined with a face lift. In other cases, it's done as a separate procedure for patients who don't need or don't want a face lift. Those who have a minimum of sagging achieve the best results. Some of the excess fat and skin are removed from the chin area, and the scar is positioned in a skin fold underneath the chin. If sagging is extensive, all the loose skin can't be removed.

Submental lipectomy is the procedure for improving a "turkey gobbler" neck. Here we make an incision beneath the chin and remove some of the fat (if too much is removed, a depression will result). Unless this surgery is performed in conjunction with a face lift, excess skin will remain.

Cleft lip and palate surgery are best begun during infancy, continuing in stages as the child develops; however, adults with no previous surgery for these deformities also can be helped. Cheiloplasty, the type of lip surgery used to correct these conditions, also can be used to make thin lips more prominent or reduce thick lips. This type of surgery is frequently performed in France but is less often requested in this country. The procedure is fairly simple. To correct thin lips, we cut away a small amount of skin beyond the red tissue of either the upper or lower lip, then move up the mucous membrane to create fuller lips. The scar is barely visible and can be easily covered with makeup. For thick lips, we make an incision inside the mouth and remove some of the lip tissue to reduce the fullness. Because this procedure is performed from inside the mouth, there are no visible scars.

Another problem that can be surgically corrected is a "gummy" smile, one in which the upper lip elevates and exposes a large area of the gums. We minimize this condition by removing some of the upper lip and gum tissue and stitching the surfaces together.

9
FINISHING TOUCHES

"Costly thy habit as thy purse can buy,
But not express'd in fancy;
  rich, not gaudy;
For the apparel oft proclaims the man."[40]

Clothes tell a story: they have a language all their own that reveals who you are, what you do, how you feel about your body and yourself. I'm often struck by the clothing my patients wear. Some hide, some assert themselves; some adhere religiously to tradition, while others follow fads that are unflattering or inappropriate. Still others look smashing, without spending a lot of money.

For most of us, clothes are more than something to put on. Knowing how to dress skillfully can be a critical factor in business and social success. For instance, some image specialists contend that television news anchorman Dan Rather "warmed up" his image by swapping the traditional suit jacket for a sleeveless V-neck pullover sweater.

Clothing also offers endless possibilities for cleverly concealing physical imperfections with taste and style. All you need are the facts about your body, occupation, and lifestyle; a few simple tricks to fool the eye; some planning and imagination; and self-esteem. Let the language of clothing speak well of you. Although the following suggestions are generally considered basics, you're the best authority on your own wardrobe—if it makes you feel good, wear it!

Instinct and common sense are the best guidelines in choosing apparel. Your biggest investment should be in the clothes you'll wear most often. For most buinesspeople, this means suits, shirts, and accessories for men and suits, dresses, blouses, and accessories for women. There's an adage in the working world: "Dress for the position you *want,* not the one you have." In addition to this consideration, your clothing should be suitable for the occasion. The following example, from a feature titled "Dress for Success" that appeared in *Savvy* magazine,[41] was written by a woman private investigator:

> Four male investigators from various agencies had failed. The client said to me, "A summons has to be served on the President of one of the top companies in Los Angeles. His office is in the penthouse. To reach him you have to pass through a lobby filled with security guards and pass the big round console with television monitors trained on elevators, halls, and offices. Take an elevator to the 18th floor, cross another lobby, heavily loaded with security guards, and take the other elevator to the top. No one knows what the man looks like, what kind of car he drives, or what hours he works. You'll earn a $100 bonus plus all the expenses if you can serve him." On Monday morning at 7:59 A.M. I parked my car in the building's garage. I had done my homework and knew that moguls have a habit of arriving early on Monday morning, then scattering like buckshot or secluding themselves in meetings for the rest of the week. I was dressed demurely, almost invisibly in a beige wool skirt, white blouse, white sweater. Nowhere along the line did anyone cast a glance at me even though I wore no pass. When the elevator stopped at the penthouse, I stepped directly in front of the receptionist's desk. "I'm here to see Mr. Big," I said.
> She was still combing her hair. "There he is," she pointed.
> When I walked up to him, he smiled at me absentmindedly and accepted the papers. Then he glanced down at them and roared: "How did you get in here?"
> "It was a cinch," I replied. "Everyone, men and women, assumes a woman dressed like this is a secretary."
> It was 8:10 A.M. when I pulled out of the garage. I had earned more than $100 in ten minutes—where all men had failed.

Although most of us don't experience such a dramatic illustration of how wearing the right clothes for the occasion brings tangible benefits, clothing is the "packaging" for the product we're trying to sell (ourselves), so we should make our selections with care. For the purposes of this book, your clothing is discussed as it relates to your face. However, your total body configuration, along with your personality, are other factors to consider in the selection process.

The same basic rules apply to men and women. A sharp eye is more important than a large budget, but buy the best clothes you can afford. Take advantage of seasonal sales to add really good clothes to your wardrobe. A few well-constructed, classically styled garments in fabrics such as wool, silk, linen, cotton, and blends of natural and synthetic fibers are a better investment than a large wardrobe of cheap, trendy outfits.

Some notes on collars: Suits with either shirts or blouses are one of the most basic forms of business attire. One thing men and women both should note carefully when selecting a suit is the jacket collar. This should fit neatly and closely, not hang away from the back of your neck. The collars of shirts and blouses that button at the neck also should fit properly—neither too tight nor too loose.

Today's rapidly changing fashion trends allow more sophistication and freedom of expression. You needn't look drab to appear businesslike. While most people in business still rely on a conservative look, clothing with a modern cut, accented by interesting but tasteful accessories, provides ample opportunity to add individuality and pizzazz to the basic work uniform, albeit subtly. Women are particularly fortunate because they have such a wide range of choices in neckline styles for blouses and dresses worn with suit jackets or blazers. A change of style can create a totally different feeling, as the photos below indicate.

Select your major items—suits or dresses—from one or two flattering and complementary color families, then mix and match for variety. Add other complementary colors and drama with shirts, blouses, and accessories. And, when choosing clothing to emphasize or camouflage, follow the principles of dark and light. Dark colors and matte finishes make an area recede; light, shiny fabrics and colors bring an area forward.

Selecting the best colors for you is very important in the impres-

sion you make on other people, says color consultant Carole Jackson, the author of *Color Me Beautiful.* "Everyone has a basic skin tone based on their inherited coloring. Two people can wear the same color and look entirely different. For one person, the selected color may enhance their skin tone, making it appear clear, smooth, and free of dark circles and lines. For the other person, the same color can detract from their skin tone, bringing out shadows, dark circles, lines, and blotches and making his or her skin look muddy. The first person is bringing out his or her best; the second looks tired and older—both while wearing exactly the same color."

The reason for this, the colorist explains, is that each of us inherits a basic skin tone that is complimented by some colors and diminished by others. Ms. Jackson and the consultants she trains divide people into four basic color categories named for the seasons:

• *Winters* have the greatest variety of types. Although they may have been blonde as a child, as adults they usually have dark hair (medium or dark brown or black), or an ash tone, but not bright red. Their skin is either extremely white or very dark (most Blacks and Orientals are in this category). There's also a middle group with either rose-beige or a sallow beige skin tone. Eyes are usually blue, green with gray tones, brown-black, or rose-brown. Examples of Winters are Elizabeth Taylor, Cher, Erik Estrada, Jacqueline Onassis, Omar Sharif, Richard Nixon, Dan Rather, Richard Simmons, and Bryant Gumble.

    Some color choices for these people are pure white, taupe, gray, black, navy, emerald green, hot pink, red, magenta, lemon yellow, purple, and ice blue.

• *Autumns* are the opposite of Winters. They may be redheads, brunettes with or without red highlights, golden blondes, or dark blondes. Their skin tone is peachy, ivory, or golden-beige. They have green eyes, often with yellow flecks, or brown eyes with a golden cast; very few have blue eyes. Examples of Autumns are Carol Burnett, Vanessa Redgrave, Shirley McLaine, Red Skelton, Robert Redford, Ann-Margret, and Katherine Hepburn.

    Some color choices for these people are oyster white, dark brown, teal blue, olive, orange, peach, red-orange, tomato red, and gold.

• *Summers* are a softer version of Winters, with a cooler skin tone. Their hair can be blonde (platinum or tow-headed as a child), ash brown, or mousy brown. They are the only season who can successfully frost their hair. The skin tone may be a bit sallow, with a translucent look to the skin. Eyes are blue most often, but also may be hazel: green with soft brown around the pupils. Examples of Summers are Farrah Fawcett, Cheryl Tiegs, Queen Elizabeth of England, Warren Beatty, Robert Wagner, Cary Grant, Johnny Carson, Jane Pauley, David Hartman, Phil Donahue, and John Davidson.

Some color choices for these people are mauve, lavender, fuchsia, light lemon-yellow, maroon, blue-red, blue-green, powder blue, and beige.

- *Springs* are the softer counterpart of Autumns and are the most delicate-looking of the seasons. Their hair may be a light red, golden blonde, or golden brown. The skin tone is ivory, peach-hued, or a light golden-beige. Their eyes are very clear, either blue or green, often with yellow flecks. Examples of Springs are Sally Struthers, Julie Andrews, Debbie Reynolds, and Jimmy Carter.

Some color choices for these people are violet, golden yellow, red-orange, aqua, tan, and camel.

If you only wear the colors that are best for you, shopping is easier and more economical because you won't waste time or money buying garments or accessories that aren't right . . . and you'll always look your best.

ACCESSORIES

Accessories, especially well-chosen jewelry, are a businesswoman's best friend. They add dash and flair to clothing, minimize flaws, and dress an outfit up or down. The same clothing can take a woman from the office to the opera with simple accessory changes. As discussed in Chapter 7, business jewelry is part of your signature and is best selected in gold or silver. Silk scarves in different lengths, widths, colors, and designs are among the most versatile accessories you can own. Many women enjoy selecting native or unusual jewelry and other accessory items as reminders of their travels—and indications of their personalities. Whatever your preferences, follow the same principles here as with clothing. You can best serve your wardrobe by investing in a few special scarves and pieces of good jewelry and other well-designed items that express your sense of style.

Just as jewelry is one of the keys to a woman's personality and style, so neckties are an important part of a man's image. For this reason, men should select their own ties to ensure that they convey the right impression. In general, you'll want to choose more conservative colors and designs for business. Silk is the best tie fabric because of its luxurious appearance. It's also the easiest fabric to knot. Wool challis or heavier weaves also are good choices. For warm weather, you might want to have a few cotton ties. In most cases, business jewelry for men still is limited to tie tacks. (Save gold or silver chains for casual wear.)

Since clothing and accessories not only frame the face but also can emphasize or detract from features, here are some guidelines for dealing with the most common problems.

1. *Round Face, Short Neck.* Wear open collars and choose bateau, wide U-neck, or long V-neck styles. Long pendant chains and low-slung scarves are good accessories. Avoid choker necklaces, cowl necklines, big frilly bows or ruffles, and harlequin collars. Wear turtlenecks only in thin material.

2. *Long Face and Neck.* Try ruffles and bow blouses, cowl and scoop necklines. Fill in necklines with scarves, heavy wide collars, necklaces, or bulky chokers. Or, wear several lengths of chains or pearls.

3. *Double Chin.* Avoid bow blouses and ruffles, dangling earrings, and chokers. Draw attention down with long scarves, long necklaces. Play up your eyes.

4. *Laugh Lines.* Hats, bright light-catching earrings (but not dangles), shoulder scarves, and long necklaces draw focus away from the mouth area. But don't stop smiling.

5. *Wrinkles Around the Lips, Crepey Neck.* Play up your eyes; wear hats, long pendants, scarves. Try soft bows, turtlenecks, and high collars.

MEN:

1. *Short Neck, Double Chin.* Wear lightweight turtlenecks; collars with a short rise and long points; thin ties and knots.

2. *Long Neck.* Select high-rise collars with short points; turtlenecks; open collars with scarves. Bow ties (if you can carry them off) or wide ties with large knots minimize this problem.

3. *Crepey Neck.* If collars and ties are too tight, they'll cut into the neck and cause skin to sag over the collar. Turtlenecks and V-neck sweaters over high collars will help disguise an aging neck.

10
HOW TO FIND PROFESSIONAL HELP

"You shall be fairer than you are."[42]

Now that you've reviewed the possibilities for improving those areas of your appearance with which you aren't totally happy, you may have decided that professional help is needed. If so, you'll be joining an ever growing number of men and women who consult specialists in order to make image changes. How do you find the right person for your image-improvement campaign?

Sometimes your hairstylist, cosmetologist, or esthetician can be a good resource, since these professionals see the results—both good and bad—of many face-altering procedures. Although it's not a guarantee that you'll obtain the same results, personal recommendation is still one of your best guides. Friends and associates who are "satisfied customers" can be good barometers of professional ability—especially if you've seen and approved of the results they got. In my experience, the majority of cosmetic-surgery patients select a doctor based on recommendations.

This shouldn't be your sole criterion, but it's a good starting point, whether you're contemplating a complete make-over by an image consultant or a few changes by a medical specialist. Here are some additional general guidelines:

200

1. Shop around. Don't settle for the first person you consult (although this specialist may be your eventual choice). Investigate at least three possible candidates. Feeling secure about the person you select is worth the extra effort—and even spending a little more money on consulting fees, if necessary. It's better to invest a bit more up front than to wind up with a large bill for results that don't please you.
2. Think about the questions you want answered prior to your consultation/inspection visit. Write them down so you won't forget anything, and if the person you're interviewing is "too busy" to give you the answers, strike him or her off your list. You have a right to know what you're buying. Some of the things you'll want to know include:

- The person's credentials, professional affiliations, training, and experience in the area for which you want assistance. While licenses and board certifications don't guarantee ability, they at least indicate some degree of training.
- Costs, including any "extras" or follow-up fees. Ask about extended payment schedules, especially if the work will be very expensive.
- Exactly what will be involved in making the changes you contemplate. Especially for medical procedures, you should have a clear understanding of what will be done and why.
- Time. How much will be necessary for the actual procedure as well as any follow-up visits?
- Possible side effects. Anything involving chemicals or medical procedures has potential risks, however small. Ask!
- What will be expected of you afterwards. When appropriate, discuss your lifestyle, your occupation, or personality factors that might influence the choices being made. For instance, if you can't be bothered with setting or other interim hairstyle maintenance procedures, you'll want a style that requires a minimum of effort on your part.
- What you can realistically expect from the expert—clearly spelled out.
- What steps will be taken to rectify unsatisfactory results. Will the problem be corrected at no additional charge to you?
- Other clients or patients with whom you can talk, if appropriate.
3. Evaluate the appearance of facilities and staff. Are the premises attractive, clean, neat, and well-organized? Do the staff members look well-groomed and seem to be efficient and pleasant?

WHO DOES WHAT?

More than one type of professional may be qualified to perform many of the appearance-enhancement procedures I've discussed—and sometimes several specialists will work together to achieve the desired results. The following is a guide to who does what:

Audiologist. Specializes in the prevention, identification, and assessment of hearing impairment in infants, young children, and adults. Provides hearing testing and hearing aid selection and fitting. Also works with auditory education in speech (lip) reading.

Barber/beautician. These terms have been supplanted by "hairstylist" and "cosmetologist."

Bariatric physician. Specializes in weight loss, gain, and maintenance.

Color consultant. Specializes in the selection of the best clothing and makeup colors for individual skin and hair colors.

Cosmetic surgeon. Plastic surgeon specializing in cosmetic procedures.

Cosmetologist. Specializes in hair cutting, styling, treatment, and coloring; skin care; and makeup application.

Dentist. Provides general dental treatment such as cleaning and filling teeth.

Dermatologist. Medical doctor specializing in the diagnosis and management of skin diseases.

Electrologist. Specializes in permanent removal of unwanted hair from the face and body.

Endodontist. Dental specialist with advanced education in treating problems with tooth pulp and root tissues.

Esthetician. Specializes in skin care; sometimes includes makeup consultations.

Exercise specialist. Organizes exercise programs for group classes; sometimes offers private instruction.

Hair colorist. Specializes in hair coloring only.

Hairdresser/stylist. Specializes in hair cutting, styling, treatment, and coloring.

Hair weaving/implant clinics. Specialize in nonmedical methods of securing hairpieces to the scalp.

Hearing-aid specialist/dealer. Specializes in testing hearing for the purpose of fitting and selling hearing aids.

Image consultant. Specializes in total image, including wardrobe, hairstyle, makeup, public presentation, and career strategy.

Laryngologist. Medical doctor specializing in diseases of the throat.

Makeup consultant. Specializes in makeup selection and proper application.

Ophthalmologist. Medical doctor specializing in the diagnosis and treatment of both vision problems and eye diseases.

Optician. Specializes in making glasses or contact lenses from prescriptions supplied by ophthalmologists or optometrists.

Optometrist. An independent health professional specializing in the diagnosis and treatment of vision problems with eyeglasses, contact lenses, or vision therapy.

Oral/maxillofacial surgeon. Dental specialist with advanced education in surgical procedures of the teeth and jaw.

Orthodontist. Dental specialist with advanced education in the prevention and correction of bad bites, crooked or badly spaced teeth, and other related problems.

Otolaryngologist. Medical doctor specializing in the diagnosis and treatment of ear, nose, and throat problems and diseases.

Otologist. Medical doctor specializing in the diagnosis and treatment of hearing problems and diseases.

Periodontist. Dental specialist with advanced education in the diagnosis and treatment of gum and oral tissue diseases.

Personal shopper. Specializes in shopping for a client's wardrobe needs and bringing selected items to the client for approval.

Plastic surgeon. Specializes in reconstructive and cosmetic procedures on all parts of the body; sometimes practice is limited to reconstructive surgery only.

Prosthodontist. Dental specialist with advanced education in replacing missing teeth with permanent or removable dentures; also performs jaw surgery.

Rhinologist. Medical doctor specializing in the diagnosis and treatment of nose problems and diseases.

Sleep clinics. Specialize in the diagnosis and treatment of sleep disorders.

Trichologist. Specializes in the diagnosis and treatment of hair problems.

The following organizations may be able to provide you with more information about and help in finding a qualified specialist in many of the above areas.

Academy of Dispensing Otologists
c/o Dr. Marlene A. Bevan
802 Garfield Avenue
Traverse City, Michigan 49684

Academy of General Dentistry
211 East Chicago Avenue
Chicago, Illinois 60611

American Academy of Dermatology
820 Davis Street
Evanston, Illinois 60201

American Academy of Facial Plastic and Reconstructive Surgery
1101 Connecticut Avenue, NW, Suite 700
Washington, D.C. 20036

American Academy of Ophthalmology
1100 17th Street, N.W.
Washington, D.C. 20036

American Academy of Otolaryngology
1100 17th Street, N.W.
Washington, D.C. 20036

American Academy of Periodontology
211 East Chicago Avenue
Chicago, Illinois 60611

American Association of Orthodontics
460 North Lindbergh Blvd.
St. Louis, Missouri 63141

American Dental Association
211 East Chicago Avenue
16th Floor
Chicago, Illinois 60611

American Optometric Association
243 North Lindbergh Blvd.
St. Louis, Missouri 63141

American Society of Plastic and Reconstructive Surgeons
233 North Michigan Avenue, Suite 1900
Chicago, Illinois 60601

Associated Master Barbers & Beauticians of America
Post Office Box 220782
Charlotte, North Carolina 28222

Cosmetic, Toiletry & Fragrance Association
1100 Vermont Avenue, N.W.
Washington, D.C. 20005

Directory of Personal Image Consultants
Editorial Services Company
1140 Avenue of the Americas
New York, New York 10036

U.S. Food and Drug Administration
8757 Georgia Avenue
Silver Springs, Maryland 20910

International Guild of Professional Electrologists, Inc.
15 Bond Street
Great Neck, New York 11021

National Association to Aid Fat Americans, Inc.
Post Office Box 43
Bellerose, New York 11426

National Hairdressers and Cosmetologists Association Inc.
3510 Olive Street
St. Louis, Missouri 63103

National Hearing-Aid Society
20361 Middlebelt
Livonia, Michigan 48152

National Society to Prevent Blindness
79 Madison Avenue
New York, New York 10016

Skin Care Association of America
c/o Kay Acuazzo
264 South 20th Street
Philadelphia, Pennsylvania 19103

FOR THE RECORD

The final step in your appearance-enhancement program should be to record the results with a good set of professional photographs. You may want these to accompany job résumés and for use with any promotional materials. Wherever your photograph appears, it's a reflection both of you and of your company, so periodically update this important image tool.

In selecting a photographer, use the same criteria discussed earlier in this chapter. Once you've chosen the photographer, discuss what you should wear. You may want to have pictures in several outfits for different uses. Also, determine where the photographs will be taken—in a studio, in your office, at some other location, or a combination of these.

Most professional photographers are adept at cosmetic touch-ups, but you should apply your makeup very carefully before arriving for the shooting. Studios don't always have good makeup lights and mirrors available. If you decide to have your makeup professionally applied before your photography session, tell the consultant exactly what you want to achieve so the makeup will be done appropriately. Your hair also should be freshly styled so you'll appear to your best advantage.

SUMMING UP

Throughout this book, I have tried to present practical suggestions for making the most of your own unique facial assets. Many of these ideas are simple changes you can achieve on your own. Others require the services of one or more of the specialists mentioned in this chapter. The goal has been to let you know your options for showing the world your best face and making a first impression that counts, personally and professionally. I hope your efforts meet with success.

References

1. Paul Schilder, *The Image and Appearance of the Human Body*, Psychological Monographs, no. 4 (London: K. Paul, Thrench, Trubner and Company, 1935), p. 267.
2. Aristotle, *Works*, vol. 4, *Historia Animalium*, trans. J. J. Baere et al. and ed. David W. Ross (Oxford: Oxford University Press, 1910).
3. Gordon W. Allport, *Personality: A Psychological Interpretation* (New York: Henry Holt & Co., 1937), pp. 67-70.
4. Ibid., pp. 69-91.
5. Roger Squier and John Mew, "The Relationship Between Facial Structure and Personality Characteristics," *The British Journal of Social Psychology* 20, no. 2 (1981): 151-60.
6. "This Is What You Thought About . . . The Impact of Beauty," *Glamour*, April 1982, p. 33.
7. American Optometric Association and Abbott Laboratories, "Your Miraculous Eyes" (St. Louis, [n.d.]).
8. Ellen Berscheid and Elaine Walster, "Physical Attractiveness," *Advances in Experimental Social Psychology,* vol. 7 (n.p., 1974), p. 207.
9. Ellen Berscheid, "An Overview of the Psychological Effects of Physical Attractiveness," *Psychological Aspects of Facial Form*, Craniofacial Growth Series monograph no. 11, (Ann Arbor, [n.d.]), p. 7.
10. Gerald R. Adams and Sharyn M. Crossman, *Physical Attractiveness: A Cultural Imperative* (Roslyn Heights, N.Y.: Libra Pubs., 1978), p. 17.
11. Stuart W. Cook, "Judgment of Intelligence from Photographs," *Journal of Abnormal and Social Psychology* 34, no. 3 (1939): 384-88.
12. Berscheid, "Overview of Psychological Effects," p. 73.
13. Elizabeth Wheeler, "The Perils of Pretty," *Working Woman*, May 1981, pp. 98-101.
14. C. H. Cooley, *Human Nature and the Social Order* (New York: Scribner Publishing, 1902), p. 97.

15. Maryland Commission on Human Relations, *Report on the Study of Weight and Size Discrimination as Directed by the Legislature of the State of Maryland in House Joint Resolution 75,* prepared by David H. Tucker, 1979, pp. 41–51.

16. Private Nationwide Survey (New York: Robert Half International, 1974).

17. "The Right Image," *Working Woman,* October 1980, p. 45.

18. The National Commission on Working Women, *Women, Work & Age Discrimination: Challenging the Workplace Myths,* prepared by Janice DeGooyer, November 1981, p. 2.

19. Berscheid and Walster, "Physical Attractiveness," p. 206.

20. Berscheid, "Overview of Psychological Effects," pp. 19–20.

21. Gerald Adams, "The Effects of Physical Attractiveness on the Socialization Process," *Psychological Aspects of Facial Form,* Craniofacial Growth Series, monograph no. 11, (Ann Arbor, [n.d.]), p. 42.

22. Berscheid, "Overview of Psychological Effects," pp. 15–17.

23. Judith Waters, "A Study of the Impact of Physical Appearance on Perceptions of Job Applicants" (New York: Clairol Corporation, 1978).

24. Henry W. Hough, *Original Object.*

25. *She Stoops to Conquer,* act 1, sc. 1.

26. James O. Stallings with Marcia Powell, *Beauty Is My Business: A Plastic Surgeon Looks at Health, Nutrition, and Exercise* (New York: Frederick Fell Publishers, 1982), pp. 163–64.

27. Ibid., p. 11.

28. Ibid., p. 37.

29. Albert M. Kligman, "The Soap Chamber Test: A New Method for Assessing the Irritancy of Soaps," *Journal of the American Academy of Dermatology* 1 (1979): 35–41.

30. U.S. Department of Commerce, *U.S. Industrial Outlook,* prepared by Leo McIntyre, 1980, p. 175.

31. Thomas Browne, *Religio Medici,* Part I; 2.

32. Norma Lee Browning, *Face-lifts* (Garden City, N.Y.: Doubleday & Co., 1982).

33. *Twelfth Night,* act 1, sc. 3, lines 96–97.

34. *Ladies Home Journal* / Clairol Survey: "How Haircolor Changed My Life," New York, 1981.

35. William Shakespeare, *Sonnets,* no. 17, lines 5–8.

36. *New York Times,* 1 March 1978, p. 10.

37. Attributed to Langford Reed.

38. National Hearing-Aid Society, "The Hearing Impaired: Facts and Figures," (Livonia, Mich., 1981).
39. Song of Sol. 4:2–4.
40. *Hamlet*, act 1, sc. 3, lines 70–72.
41. Rosemary Breckler, "Dressed for Success," *Savvy*, April 1982, p. 87.
42. *Anthony and Cleopatra*, act I, sc. 2, line 18.

Index

214